UNTETHERED

A MEMOIR

Published in Canada, for Global Distribution by YGTMedia Co.

www.ygtmedia.co
For more information email: info@ygtmedia.co

ISBN trade paperback: 978-1-998754-66-3
eBook: 978-1-998754-67-0

To order additional copies of this book:
info@ygtmedia.co

UNTETHERED

A MEMOIR

THE STORY OF HOW I LOST
MY RELIGION TO FIND MY VOICE

AMBER POWERS

TABLE OF CONTENTS

Dedication 01

Foreward 03

Chapter 1: Life in a Rabbit Hole 05

Chapter 2: A Puddle of Tears 21

Chapter 3: Will I Ever Go Home? 45

Chapter 4: My Mad Wedding Party 57

Chapter 5: Reflections Through the Looking Glass 75

Chapter 6: Curiouser 85

Chapter 7: Behind the Veil 105

Chapter 8: Amber's Evidence 129

Chapter 9: Find Your Wonderland 143

Acknowledgments 149

DEDICATION

To the five-year-old, twelve-year-old, and seventeen-year-old me who wanted so desperately to fit in. . . . My love, you were meant to stand out. You were divinely and purposefully created for the mission only you could carry out. You are stronger than you know. You are a beacon of hope. You are love embodied. Stand proudly, Amber. You're going to change the world—one human at a time.

FOREWORD

When I said yes to writing just a portion of my story, I had to ask myself, "Why? Why now? Why me? And most importantly, for whom?"

While writing this book certainly brought natural catharsis for me, it's also a tool for you. No matter who you are or where you come from, if you've found this book, it was on purpose.

You'll see references to *Alice in Wonderland* in this book. That is on purpose. Alice was an escape for me. Her ups and downs (literally and figuratively), her wandering through a strange land filled with outlandish characters—it just made sense to me. Her constant search for her way back home reminded me of finding my way to my center, to myself.

Over time, I saw and read multiple iterations of her story. I got lost in her adventures. I was there with her as she overcame her fears of the Jabberwocky, Jubjub Bird, and the Bandersnatch. It was perhaps the fictional stories created about a real-life girl from the late 1800s that taught me the importance of letting fear take a back seat in my life. And that one lesson has been a true north star that has led me to be the woman I am today.

As you read through the pages ahead, you will see representations of characters and situations that may have been changed. Know that while the details may be altered for legal reasons, the outcome and lessons learned are all very much the same as my actual life experiences.

My hope is that as you comb through the pages ahead, you'll find the courage to do the hard things, you'll learn to trust your intuition, and you'll gather the strength to say yes to yourself, even when society says you have to follow a certain path to gain acceptance and love.

I'm cheering you on every step of the way.

CHAPTER 1:
LIFE IN A RABBIT HOLE

In the fall of 1978, as I obliviously toddled toward my second birthday, more than 900 people died in the Jonestown Massacre in Guyana, South America. Two of the people who died were relatives I would never get the chance to know. On the other side of my family, my great-grandmother pulled her family from Jones's church when she had a gut feeling something dark was at work.

The church my parents attended when I was born was visited by Jim Jones, the leader of the cult that led to the Jonestown massacre. At that time, Jones was known for visiting local Indianapolis churches near his own and inviting the members to his church.

While I would never personally know Jim Jones or his congregation members, this set the stage for what was to become the first nearly thirty years of my life. Both sets of my grandparents joined a different cult than the one Jones led, and my parents met at this other cult. I am now untethering myself from decades' worth of programming I wholeheartedly embraced in that same cult.

As a young child, I had no reason to question my parents'— and hence, my—choice of faith. In my young mind, everyone everywhere just went to different locations of the same church. They might meet at different times or on different days, but my naivety said we were all being taught the same thing. Outwardly, I couldn't see the differences between myself, our church members, and the rest of the world. I was allowed to wear pants and shorts like any other child, but on Sundays, we went full-out Sunday best. For girls my age, this meant we were swallowed in frilly dresses. Lace surrounded my ankles that rested right above my patent leather Mary Janes.

My time at home was spent playing with Strawberry Short-cake as I listened to the adventures of her and Blueberry Muffin on my 45 record player. Every time the record chimed, I was trained to turn the page. I fell asleep to my Sesame Street night-light that cast a dim hue from the ledge of my windowsill.

I ran bare-chested and carefree across our five acres, chasing wild rabbits for long enough my parents finally caved in and got my brother and me our own bunnies: Jenny and Petey. We had a Chesapeake Bay Retriever named Chessie I adored, and a cow named Scottie I later learned became our dinner. Most of our acreage was a garden I would help my grandpa tend, and by "tend," I mean I'd pull up the green onions as soon as he planted them.

If I wasn't running around on our land, chasing the neighbor's peacocks, or listening to my old-school audiobooks, I was likely at my other grandparents' house fishing or "hunting Indian arrowheads" as my paternal grandmother would tell me.

"Your great-great-great-grandfather was an Indian Chief, you know."

I had her share this story with me again and again as I grew older, prying for more information every time she told it, but never getting very far.

"That information was lost in the Trail of Tears," she'd say. Disappointed, I'd find myself later in life trying to connect with the Native roots she spoke of.

When I was a preschooler, my extended family often visited our home. As is the case with most children, my natural inclination was to trust my family. This trust is a false security blanket many parents and guardians unwittingly instill in their children. My earliest memories of time spent with extended family members are filled with sexual abuse. I remember hearing the front door swinging open and the spirited pleasantries beginning. That was always my cue. I'd tiptoe my way across the floorboards so they wouldn't squeak. *Maybe they would just peek in my room, not see me, and look somewhere else.* I'd then slowly and methodically close my sliding wood closet doors. I'd take a deep breath in . . . and slowly exhale so not to make too much noise. The baby blue walls of that closet felt like they were closing in around me as I'd clutch my knees to my chest and pray to God they wouldn't find me.

This was my first memory of trying to make myself smaller so I couldn't be found, trying to make my entire self silent. But it didn't matter; no matter how small I made myself, and no matter how quiet I was, I was always found.

Anytime a relative (of any gender, since I was abused by both males and females) came near me for a kiss, panic would fill my body. Finally, on one day when one of my cousins approached me asking for a kiss, I couldn't take the stress any longer. While this cousin was never one who assaulted me, his approach caused me to sob uncontrollably. Consumed by fear, I couldn't keep quiet. After telling my mom about what had been occurring, stayovers with extended family halted, and my abuse at their hands finally came to an end.

But sleepovers with church friends continued. And even there, some of my female church friends also wanted to explore my body by "playing doctor." This was like no doctor's visit I'd ever been to, and as an adult, I know this isn't a natural game young children know how to play without being taught. It felt wrong, but I wanted to be liked and accepted, so I let it continue for a short while. As an eight-year-old, my sexuality had been tainted by no fewer than six people, four of whom were significantly older than I was—nearly adults. While the first sexual assaults were frightening and caused me to feel ashamed of myself, by the age of eight, it had sadly become the norm.

I thought this was how to seek attention and love, but at the same time, it was around this time I started acting out when I sensed, heard, or saw my parents showing any form of intimacy. Rage would build in me to the point where I wanted to scream at the top of my lungs. For years I'd act out in my rage by breaking them up mid-kiss or banging on their bedroom door. They didn't understand what was happening, and, quite frankly, neither did I until I went through therapy as an adult.

As I grew older, I began to seek deeper knowledge about God, or at least that's how I framed it at the time. What I really wanted to know, however, was everything I wasn't being told, by both the church and the people I looked to as leaders. There were so many mysteries. Often, when my parents went shopping at the mall, they'd let me stay in the B. Dalton bookstore to look around. They didn't know it, but as soon as they'd leave, I'd plant myself in the theology section and read everything I could get my hands on. I read everything from Hal Lindsey (an evangelical dispensationalist) to witchcraft books about spells (which I kept a secret because I had been taught it was wrong and felt ashamed for even opening such a book).

One time I went into a bookstore that had a Satanist Bible. Now, I was made to feel as though anything other than believing in our sect of Christianity would doom me to hell. But a Satanist Bible? I was sure I would burst into flames if I even touched it. I contemplated for five minutes whether I should open it, but then walked away and looked at some other sections of the store, the Satanic Bible in the back of my mind the whole time. Taking a deep breath, I concluded, *Well, if I die, it'll be quick, so just rip off the Band-Aid.* I walked back to it, opened it to the first page, and scanned the contents while holding my breath. When finished, I quickly closed the book and exhaled. I hadn't died, but I didn't want to tempt fate.

On Sundays, most of my biological family converged at church. My paternal grandmother was the first Sunday School teacher I remember. She taught me the books of the Bible and about the apostles. I had to memorize them all. She was also the children's music teacher as well as a choir member. Being in the choir, she could get a good view of the congregation, and she took particular note of two deaf people who would occasionally attend church services.

For our Christmas program that year, she asked me to learn how to sign "Silent Night" so I could sign the lyrics while the children's choir performed it. I agreed, but I had no clue how to teach myself. So, I went to the bookstore and found a sign language dictionary with rudimentary arrows showing how to move your hands. I was unaware at the time that American Sign Language has its own syntax, so I looked each word up individually and placed it in the English word order. I then practiced a few words at a time until I had an entire stanza memorized before moving on to the next. After weeks of practice, I was finally ready to stand in front of the congregation. I was so nervous. I had a feeling I was doing the signs all wrong and was about to be found out.

Standing on the platform in my white bedsheet converted into an angel costume, with a tinsel halo hovering above my head, I began signing while the children's choir sang. And as I stared out into the congregation, there were two pairs of eyes staring back at me intently. After the program was complete, I learned one of our church families had a deaf niece and nephew. I felt for the first time in my life like the role I played in that Christmas program mattered for something.

I used to gaze at my paternal grandmother in the choir box from the congregation, thinking how beautiful she was. She was a tall woman with a large athletic frame, reddish skin, high cheekbones, and coal-black hair. Her voice was strong, and she always sang with a bluegrass twang, having come from the hills of Virginia.

My maternal grandmother was the "head cook" of our church kitchen, a role that would later be passed on to my mother. I'd often sit up on the cold, stainless-steel kitchen prep table with a can opener as big as my head opening one giant can of tomato sauce after another. It was in her kitchens, the one at church and the one in our home on that five-acre farm, where I learned my love of cooking and baking.

Our Sundays began with Sunday School, an hour-long lesson for children five to thirteen. This was followed by the Sunday afternoon service, which typically consisted of music and worship. Most Sunday afternoons included a "prayer line" that had women line up on one side of the sanctuary while men lined the other side. We sometimes whispered our prayer to the minister; other times we chose to keep our prayer request silent. The minister then placed hands on our foreheads and prayed, occasionally quite loudly, for our request.

Prayer came next, sometimes while kneeling at the altar in quiet contemplation, and sometimes by speaking in tongues, singing, dancing "in the spirit," and even marching around the pews in the sanctuary. As the prayer time came to a close, the minister would lead the congregation in Bible study or a sermon about what the world and other religious sects wanted us to believe (and all the reasons they were wrong and we were right). More often, however, the minister spoke about church history or dogma. And a couple times a year, we would have what felt like pledging auctions.

Pledging was my most dreaded time of the year because I was bored to tears. Instead of participating or paying attention, I'd get on the church floor with a piece of paper and draw or color or would build castles out of the Tart n Tinys my brother and I got from the gas station before the start of church. As I matured, I began to feel like there was something very wrong with how our pledging of tithes was done. Pledge cards were passed around, and congregation members would stand up and publicly announce how much they would pledge for a certain period of time. Even as a child, I noticed that those who gave more had more power. They were able to break the biblical or moral code we were held to without being called out.

The afternoon Sunday service tended to last a couple of hours, then we'd have a two-hour break to have an early dinner before making our way back for Sunday evening, which started with a short worship and music service followed by the testimonies of church members. Then the minister would give a short "word"—sometimes he spoke from the Bible, but mostly he spoke about how our church was right and the rest of the world was wrong, or about our church history. On some nights there was a short break between testimonies for youth group to sing or men's quartet, then we'd finish the evening with a longer, more rambunctious worship service. While most Sunday night services wrapped up by 9:30 p.m., it was not all that unusual to get home at midnight or later from a service when "the Spirit was moving." As a choir member, I could see a plaque on the pulpit that read *Watch the Spirit.* Our church leaders were taught to watch the Spirit and lead the services based on how it moved.

It was often toward the end of our Sunday night services when those not baptized in the Holy Spirit (as evidenced by not having the ability to speak in tongues) would "tarry for the Holy Spirit." I'd stand on the women's side of the church, with one woman on each side of me, extending my arms toward the heavens as if begging God to pour out on me the gift of speaking in tongues. It was only those who had this gift who would have a chance at reaching Heaven, as per our church doctrine.

With tears rolling down my cheeks, I would beg God to baptize me with this gift, often with one of the elder church women screaming in my ear to pray harder. Everyone I'd heard speaking in tongues seemed to speak in some sort of Latin language, so unless God planned on also magically gifting me with the ability to roll my Rs, I knew I was screwed. So, on one Sunday afternoon service, I faked it to get the woman yelling in my ear to stop. I played the newly baptized role quite well. Both my parents and the entire church family were so proud to welcome me into the fold of elite members.

We had many churches all over the States, and I'd heard we even had a few churches in different countries. A couple times a year, our churches from the US would convene in Louisville, Kentucky, for a general convention. One year, our family met up with Tenneva's family (Tenneva's my cousin and first best friend) in Louisville a day before the convention was to start, and our mothers took us dress shopping for the big spectacle. One frilly dress after another flew over my head. My legs, back, and waist were red from those heinous crinolines, each one a little fuller and itchier than the last.

Being strapped for cash didn't seem to enter my mom's mind that day because one elaborately frilly dress with a crinoline and lace anklets totaled an amount that resulted in an animated conversation between my mom and dad on the way to church the next day. When you're surviving on a diet of "beanie weenies" (hot dogs cut up into pork and beans), powdered milk, and Spam, the last thing she should have been spending money on was expensive dresses. But at least I was dressed in a way that would make my mom proud. We entered the massive church hand in hand. Bows adorning my freshly curled hair, I was dressed head to toe like a perfect baby doll. I learned early on that appearances were everything, something that would become the defining sentiment of the next few decades of my life.

After moving away from the first home I remembered as a child, my once-blended family (we had lived with my maternal grandparents) moved to a mobile home park in central Indiana. It was there where I'd have my first kiss, smoke my first cigarette, and make my first best friend outside of the church. It was with that best friend I'd see my first film in a movie theater, although it wasn't without a fight. Television and movies were no-no's in our church. But after making a pretty good argument ("It is just *Mickey's Christmas Carol.* How bad could it be?"), I was allowed to go.

It was also while we lived in that mobile home park that I attempted my first rebellious act. In our church, there were more "do nots" than in other churches. As a grade 1 student, I started noticing I was different. Other than the fact I was a foot taller than every other child in the class, I was also one of the few girls who didn't have her ears pierced. And once I noticed this distinction, I started noticing pierced ears everywhere. I even saw babies with little earrings. Why couldn't I have my ears pierced? My dad told me the Bible verse that stated we couldn't and it was wrong, but that still didn't make sense to me since nearly everyone I knew at school was Christian. This was one of the first awakenings I had that our church was different. When I asked why we followed different rules, I was told we were to stand out from the rest of the world. We were "called" to be different. Our bodies were to be temples—and who puts holes in the Temple of God?

But I was tired of being different, so on a bus ride home from school during grade 2, I decided to take the advice of a grade 3 girl from our mobile home park. She was older, after all . . . so I was sure she knew what she was talking about.

"All you have to do is take a piece of ice and numb your ear. You'll have to keep it on there for a while so you don't feel it when the needle goes through. Then take a raw potato and put it behind your earlobe. With your other hand, take a needle and just push it through."

On the day I made the big decision to pierce my ears, I searched our home for a needle but came up short. A safety pin would have to suffice. I iced my earlobe, cut a potato in half, and bit down on my bottom lip as hard as I could. *Here we go!* I could hear the pop of skin as the safety pin made its way through my earlobe. It wasn't as easy as I thought it was going to be. Every time I heard the pin pop through another layer of cartilage, I got a little more grossed out and a little more scared about what was going to happen if my mom found out. A close second in the fear race was being denied entry into Heaven after she killed me, since this was the biggest "sin" my young mind could conjure up.

I made it through one ear with that safety pin, but it was torturous enough to know I didn't want to do the other one. Plus, I didn't even have an earring. It wasn't exactly my most well-planned excursion to Sinner Town! So, I cleaned up the blood, and my hair was long enough my parents didn't notice what I'd done. Despite it all, I still desperately wanted pierced ears.

"As soon as I turn eighteen, I'm getting them pierced."

"Not if you're under our roof, you won't!"

That single act of rebellion led to more rebellion. While my parents were at work, I snuck the heavy utility scissors from our junk drawer in the kitchen and cut my hair. Based on our church's teaching, "But if a woman have long hair, it is a glory to her: for her hair is given her for a covering" (1 Corinthians 11:15), this was a sin. Later, I befriended the preteen boy who lived across the street from us. His mom and dad were truck drivers and were gone often. When they weren't home, I'd sneak over to his house and smoke his parents' cigarettes. And he'd sneak anything sexual he wanted from me.

My spirit was rejecting everything I was being taught. We weren't really supposed to befriend people from outside our "brand" of churches, but seeing as I was a public school student and living in a mobile home park, I could hardly avoid socialization. I didn't necessarily see my friends as bad, but it had been indoctrinated into me to "bring people into the fold"—we were to evangelize people and grow our congregations.

It was also expected that congregation members ask permission for where to vacation, whether we could go to the mall, what wedding gowns we could purchase, and what was acceptable in terms of adorning our bodies. The hard-and-fast rules for girls included: skirts past your knees, tops with high necklines and long sleeves (elbows are hella sexy, you know!), no tattoos, no alcohol, no drugs, no piercings of any kind, hair long, and no makeup. And once one hit adulthood, meaning becoming married, she wore her hair up.

If we wanted to do the things my friends outside of the church did, like get a television or go to the movies, the decision was considered by viewing the request through the lens of what the church (thus, God) would think and approve of.

In some ways, my family rebelled alongside me. We always had a TV, but what we watched on that television was highly scrutinized. I don't know what my parents watched after bedtime, but we didn't even have cable until I was a junior in high school. I was permitted to wear pants and shorts as a child, while others my age were only allowed to wear skirts and dresses. Many of our church members saw this as too lenient, which was more confusing than anything to my child's mind. I didn't understand why we were being taught one thing at church and living another way at home. *Why did we have to abide by some rules, but not all of them?*

Trying to make sense of the dichotomy between my family and my church would keep me in a constant state of confusion for years.

CHAPTER 2:
A PUDDLE OF TEARS

In school, my teachers began noticing I was different from the other kids, and not just because of my height. I remember my grade 2 teacher calling in three other teachers to see how I held a pencil to write and turned my pad of paper when I wrote. Instead of having the notepad facing me, I was turning it ninety degrees to the right, as it felt more natural to my hands. As the teachers crouched over my desk, my face became flushed and sweat started to form around my hairline. They were gawking. I slunk down in my chair, completely humiliated, while the rest of the class looked my way.

It was around this time I started to fall behind academically. I came home one afternoon with low marks on my report card. Meanwhile, my brother's marks indicated he was at the top of his class. I waited to show my mom my marks because I knew how she'd react. After my brother's report card was discovered, I knew it was only a matter of time before she asked for mine. I made my way to the dinette in the kitchen and slowly slid my report card over to her.

That was the first time she struck me across my face. She hit me so hard that the blow knocked me down. My breath left my body, and grief consumed me. No matter how hard I tried, I couldn't find the air my body needed.

"Get up! Quit being so dramatic! I didn't even hit you that hard."

My mom had a habit of whispering under her breath, and I'd become a professional at listening to decipher what was being said in those whispers. "Why can't you just be more like your brother?"

My heart hit my stomach, and my breath returned to me. "I wish I was never born!"

It was the first of many times I said and meant these words, and every time I said them, it was dismissed as me "being dramatic."

Unbeknownst to me, my parents had been talking with my teachers about my performance—or lack thereof—in school. By this time, I had stopped turning in my homework. Instead, I'd been stuffing the worksheets into my books or wadding them up and shoving them into the back of my desk where they were found during our every-other-week desk cleaning. It would later be clear to me that I have pathological demand avoidance, a pattern of avoiding work demanded of me due to the anxiety and overwhelm it causes, and this is my first memory of its detrimental effects.

One day after I got off the bus, my parents prepared us a quick dinner and then informed me we were going back to school. Anxiety set in. Parent–Teacher conferences never went well for me, and this felt like another one. But this trip to school turned out differently. Mom and Dad had tried to console me on the way there, but I was skeptical. We arrived and I was escorted into a long, narrow room with a conference table. I sat on one side and faced an unfamiliar adult.

"Am I in trouble?" I asked.

"No, Amber. You're not in trouble. You're here to take some tests so that we know how to help you do well in school."

I only partially believed her. I was petrified my mom was going to start yelling at me for being a disappointment as soon as we got back in the car to go home. But I cooperated. There were a lot of pattern-type questions I can only assume were IQ questions, and questions asking which item didn't belong with the rest.

Of course, now I know I was being tested to see if I had any learning disabilities. What the tests determined, however, was that I was bored out of my skull. I wasn't being challenged, so I was tuning out my teachers and not doing any homework. In fact, I did so well on the tests it was recommended I move ahead two grade levels. But even though I was the same height as the grade 4 students, my parents ultimately decided I wasn't emotionally mature enough to advance. The emotional gap between grade 2 and grade 4 was less like a gap and more like a chasm. And now that I've learned about autism as an adult, I'm 100 percent convinced I'm neurodivergent.

Between grades 2 and 5, I went to three different grade schools. While we always had a roof over our heads, food on the table, and clothes on our backs, money was frequently tight. Seeking a better life for their kids, Mom and Dad wanted to move out of the mobile home and into a single-family house.

Halfway into my grade 3 year, we moved to Martinsville, Indiana. There was a home close to my paternal grandparents for sale on contract, and my parents had their hearts set on it. Complete with a basement, huge kitchen, enormous bedrooms, and a great yard, it seemed too good to be true.

It was there in that house I would first be introduced to the tale of a curious and somewhat rebellious girl who never felt like she fit in with those around her, both physically and emotionally: *Alice in Wonderland*. In the 1985 made-for-TV movie, featuring an all-star cast, Alice is portrayed as a proper young English girl. Her hair is pristine, and she's dressed like a doll, complete with crinoline and tights. Alice was most concerned about being treated like a grown-up, discovering who she really was, and finding her way back home.

She was resilient and stubborn and not afraid to use her voice, even when she found herself in a strange land. If I were to pick a sister in this life, it would have been Alice. While internally, I was rebelling in my own way, it was hidden from the rest of the world. Alice was my muse. She was an escape for me. She commanded respect and was clever and witty. Alice made me want to be the same, but that took courage I wouldn't find for decades.

Alice was a girl who grew to the size of a building and then shrunk to the size of a mouse, and I understood her. I understood standing out due to my physical size, and I understood shrinking because I learned very early on that shrinking was exactly what was expected of me to fit societal "norms." As an adult looking back on these moments of shrinking and standing out, I'm not surprised *Alice in Wonderland* resonated with me so deeply.

It wasn't just my height that drew attention. From the age of eight, I was accustomed to stepping on a scale. My first memory and every memory thereafter at the doctor revolved around my height and my weight. I was so much taller than others my age, so naturally, I weighed more too. My mom and dad always joked that as a baby, I could outeat my dad. They used to laugh at that a lot. Before I was even ten years old, I accompanied my mom, her two sisters, and my grandmother to weight-loss classes. Although there were no other children—or even teenagers—in that class, I was permitted to attend to "just observe."

Now completely moved into our new home in Martinsville, Indiana, we were just a few miles away from my paternal grandmother and grandfather. I quickly learned we were also in a place heavily involved in a political war. Many powerful politicians historically from that area were not okay with Black folks.

I had been introduced to Black skin in two ways in grade 3. There was the solitary and very tall—six foot seven(ish)—Black man who went to our Louisville church. I related to him because of his size, and he made me pay closer attention to him due to our similarities. He was also quiet like me, which made me want to know him even more. After an outburst from my brother caught his attention during church, I was able to meet him. He introduced himself, and we sought him out every time we went to Louisville for a meeting after that.

My first historically accurate connection to Black people occurred in the elementary gymnasium of that same Martinsville School. Our whole grade 3 class gathered on Martin Luther King Jr. Day to watch a movie called *The Underground Railroad*. I remember crying a puddle of tears through almost the entire film wondering what would make people feel like they could treat others so cruelly. I thought, *If I had been alive during that time, I would have participated in the Underground Railroad. I would have housed slaves so they could find their freedom.*

Alice was starting to make an impact. I came home and shared the heinous events of slavery with my family. Surely they didn't know what had happened, because if they did, they would have done something about it. Or they would have told me about it already. I was using my voice for the first time, in opposition to power. As I shared my story with my mom and dad, they smiled sideways at one another—a smile I would become all too familiar with throughout my life. It was that sort of knowing grin that says, "Oh shit. We've got a spitfire on our hands."

It turns out the house in Martinsville was, in fact, too good to be true. It was infested with termites and was going to cost a small fortune to treat. So, the hunt for new housing was on. We ended up in a town named Whiteland, Indiana, for my next year of school. We rented a two-bedroom house on a busy road where I taught myself to do cartwheels in the back and side yards. My brother and I each had our own rooms with a shared bathroom. My parents' bedroom was set up in what would normally have been the dining room.

This was my first time attending an open-concept school; there were no walls separating one classroom from the next— only movable panels with open ceilings. It was a miserable failure of a concept for a girl who couldn't chew gum and walk at the same time. It was impossible to listen to my math instruction while the history teacher next door was showing a film strip on the basics of democracy.

It was also during this year I experienced the most significant death of my young life. My dad lost an aunt and uncle who were the same age as he and my mom. Every Christmas we'd gather at their home or a relatives' home who lived close by. Just the Christmas prior to their car accident, all of our cousins gathered in their attic making prank phone calls to ask neighbors if their refrigerator was running, because . . . you know . . . they'd better go catch it.

That same Christmas, we grabbed twin-sized mattresses and slid down the attic stairs. Snow be damned. We didn't need no stinking snow. It was a time I looked forward to every year. But following their accident and every year after that, our family holidays were no longer the same. It was almost as if the joy had been ripped from the heart of our family.

I sobbed for weeks after learning about their death. I couldn't put into words why I felt the way I did. What I did know was that I thought my aunt and uncle were the coolest people—but they were considered the "black sheep" of the family since they didn't attend church, nor did their actions align with what many of our family members deemed Christian behavior. I'm sure, subconsciously, I wondered whether I would see them again in Heaven since they weren't active members of our church.

Soon after the death of my great-aunt and great-uncle, my parents decided it was time to buy a home instead of renting that Whiteland two-bedroom for another year. The summer before I entered grade 5, we started looking at homes with land in the Martinsville area. There were two houses I still remember refusing to walk into because I could sense a malevolent spirit attached to both homes. My parents dismissed my intuitive nudges as ridiculous but allowed me to stay outside in the car. After very insistently declaring that if they chose to buy either house I would move in with my maternal grandparents, the search continued. They knew I was serious.

Not too far from Martinsville was a bustling town of 1,600 people in Bargersville, Indiana. While looking at a house for sale by a realtor in that town, I spotted a house across the street for sale by the owner. It was cute and stood out from the rest of the cookie-cutter houses in that neighborhood.

My parents were able to see that house soon after. Other than the green shag carpet and the dark wood panels that adorned the walls, it was perfect. This move placed us into an affluent school system significantly closer to our church. Now, while the school system itself was affluent, we were not. My mother worked in an administrative role for a Japanese company, and my dad was starting his climb up the rungs of what would be his career as a mechanical engineer.

We lived in the affordable part of the district, but I didn't really realize it until the following year when the (then) four elementary schools across the district merged into a single middle school. The social side of my school career up until grade 5 was pretty mild. I wasn't popular. I wasn't really anything other than tall, and smart. I just sort of blended in—except in the ways I stood out. Walking in the first day as a grade 5 student who looked like a senior in high school, I captured the attention of the popular kids at Maple Grove Elementary School.

I was five foot eight, wore a size 34B bra, and was all legs. While I was oblivious to it at the time, I'm sure I had the attention of some of the boys in class. It was clear to me on just the first day who the popular girls were and who their queen bee was. That's why I was shocked when she approached me and invited me to her birthday sleepover. Little did I know that the queen bee lived just down the street from me, so my parents approved.

During Sunday School, my teachers had warned us about popular games of the time that were "of the devil," but I didn't ever think I'd come face-to-face with them. Dungeons and Dragons was strictly forbidden, as it was thought to cause demonic possession. Ouija board stories of burning and having the boards return in the homes where they belonged were etched into my memory. They also talked about something called Light as a Feather, Stiff as a Board that had a small group of people use only two fingers each to lift a person lying on their back. Once in the air, everyone would remove their fingers and the person would supposedly float.

On the night of the sleepover, not only did the queen bee break out a bag of airline-size bottles of liquor for us to drink, but once we were all good and schnockered, she also insisted we try Light as a Feather, Stiff as a Board. And that shit worked! Talk about a fear spiral! Drinking and seeing someone float? I could have sworn I saw a little devil with a pitchfork dancing just outside one of the windows! Then, when the Ouija board was suggested, I suddenly "got sleepy" and refused to "play."

Soon after that night, we got a call from the queen bee's mom who stated I wasn't allowed to come over anymore. Before school, I'd been walking to her house to catch the bus, but that had to stop. I still don't know what happened, but I will say that within our church, we were encouraged to be very vocal about our faith and to remain pure and holy. While I don't remember saying anything to her about her daughter's attempt to bring upon my spiritual demise, my training to take a stand for my faith, paired with my lack of social etiquette skills, probably made for the perfect storm that resulted in the queen bee's mom's desire to end our friendship.

We were settling into our new home, getting to know neighbors, and, of course, attending church. From our house, we could arrive there in about twenty minutes, which was quite a welcome relief compared to the almost hour-long drive we'd had from our other homes. Soon, because of the short distance to church, Saturday night services became a regular occurrence, and our attendance on Wednesday night services became increasingly more frequent.

I was still attending Sunday School, which had become lessons on how to sit in the pews in a way that did not draw attention to our backsides. We were taught not to cross our legs when we sat with the congregation or on the platform to keep the men from seeing up our dresses. Plus, we were taught, it increased the chances of varicose veins. We were to have a certain poise, and after enough praise for doing things the right way, I became the prize student—a proper young woman, even.

My truest friends during this time were the ones I had made at church. They were the only ones who really understood me. It was also during this time that our church began talking about starting its own school since our doctrine was so different from that of other Christian churches. While the word *sheltered* usually has negative connotations in today's culture, the very essence of this word conveys protection. I felt a sense of safety by belonging to our church—it was like I received a warm hug every time I walked through the church doors. I couldn't find that sense of safety anywhere else. So, each week during Sunday School, I'd ask my teachers for an update on when the school would open. I longed to feel normal—to fit in.

When the announcement came that the church wouldn't be opening the school after all, every hope I had of feeling "normal" was gone. I was drowning in a pool of hopelessness. Each time I'd surface to catch my breath, I was pulled back under. I made a plea to my parents to allow me to drop out of school or to start home schooling. But no. A public school education was my only option.

For most of my life I'd felt it next to impossible to be accepted … to be seen as "normal." With a single step through those church doors, however, I only had to follow a set of rules to be loved and accepted. In reflection, I now see it was similar conditioning or training people do with their dogs: we provide praise when they act the way we expect. And that's the danger of seeking acceptance from outside sources—we can be made to do and feel something through programming.

The summer before I started middle school, my mom had a conversation with me. "Amber, you're turning into an adult, and with these changes comes a decision to dress more modestly. I'm giving you the choice to dress how you like, but remember that if we're seen out in public, you'll be expected to be dressed modestly."

For the first couple of years after that conversation, I complied and wore dresses past my knees and long-sleeved shirts with high necklines, just like my mother and the other adult women at church. Because I was a proper young Pentecostal girl, I gave away my jeans and tank tops, and I wouldn't wear that style of clothes again until high school.

My preteen body looked more like the body of a sixteen-year-old model, though, no matter how I dressed it. And the more my body developed, the more I learned to hate it. It was always under scrutiny. When I was five, my mother inappropriately called attention to my forming breasts in front of company. At eight, I was already dieting. At ten, while comparing weight at the community pool with my girlfriends who were all a foot or more shorter than I was, I earned the name "Fifth-Grade Fatty." At thirteen, I was told by my paternal grandmother I was too fat to wear leggings and that my 150-pound body might sink the Jon Boat on her lake.

Regardless, I remember confidently putting on my first bikini at four years old. I wouldn't wear another bikini until I was thirteen. We were at a relative's lake house, and when I put on that bikini, I felt like I'd just donned a prom dress. I was primed and ready to hear the compliments I was positive were coming my way only to hear my mother tell me, in a loud voice, how everyone thought I didn't have the body for it. Defeat poured over me. It was at that moment self-doubt and self-loathing really made their grand entrance. A dark and empty numbness consumed me. It became clear nothing that was the essence of me, my spirit, was of any worth. Appearances—that's the only thing I had to lean on, plus a god who seemed eager to see me fail and be doomed to hell. (I should point out that our church didn't teach a literal hell; it was the Hal Lindsey books I'd read as a young child that conjured images and fear of hell and brimstone.)

I no longer needed anyone to tell me how disgusting my body was. I grew to hate the pooch in my lower belly. I did scissor kicks, leg raises, and oblique exercises. I swam. I literally walked in place in my room every day, methodically counting steps in my head until I hit at least 8,000 steps.

Even though I had an average body, I saw a 300-pound woman staring back at me in the mirror. No one spoke about body dysmorphia at the time, but that's exactly what I was experiencing. As a teenager, I went through phases when I would only eat half a cheese sandwich per day, then the next day, I would binge and purge. I'd heard my mom doing it through the bathroom door, so I figured it couldn't be that bad for you.

Shortly after my thirteenth birthday, I started to have eyes for a young man at church. I was now considered a young adult, which meant I no longer had to sit with my parents during the services. I could sit with the youth group, which consisted of a horny lot of young adults concentrated into about 200-square feet. The ministers and leaders in the church probably thought that keeping us in different pews based on gender would dilute the hormones, but they couldn't have been more wrong.

In between our Sunday afternoon and Sunday evening services, the youth would congregate in the back pews on the north side of our church. Ushers would patrol that area to ensure no funny business was going on. "A Bible's length between you. Leave space for Jesus," they'd say.

During these brief intervals that would pass far too quickly, I found out four things about myself as it pertains to romantic attraction:

1. I love a guy with a sense of humor.
2. There's nothing sexier than a guy who isn't afraid to challenge the status quo and speak boldly about it.
3. Intelligence is a massive turn-on.
4. Bad, bad boys . . . they make me feel so good.

That first young man who caught my eye was Simon Haines. As many young girls did at the time, I'd daydream about him all through social studies, and during math, I'd calculate our chances of being married. In study hall, I'd doodle "the future Mrs. Simon Patrick Haines" all over my notebooks.

It was also during this time my mother started buying me bridal magazines, which I assumed was totally normal. Many girls I knew at that age talked about their dream wedding. They talked about the perfect floral arrangements, the perfect dress, and the perfect honeymoon destination. In my mind, I had the whole thing planned out—groom and all.

I was a smitten kitten. Months went by, and I finally got Simon's attention. I fell a little deeper with every laugh and leaned toward a possible future with him whenever I heard him buck authority. He stopped me in my tracks each time he made me question what I thought I believed. He was exactly what I wanted. He was attentive, winking at me from the band box (he played cornet) while I sat as close as I could without being obvious. We weren't allowed to hold hands, but my heart skipped a beat whenever he "accidentally" brushed my hand.

I know what most people think about young love, but I remember how I felt about Simon. It wasn't puppy love. I think puppy love is reserved for people who are permitted to toy around with young love. For teens in our church, however, young love usually resulted in permanent love, or at least an attempt at permanent love.

When Valentine's Day came, Simon got me a card and a plush heart that played "Let Me Call You Sweetheart." I swooned. He was four years my senior, which may not seem like a big gap as an adult, but as a thirteen-year-old, it meant being the age of consent . . . and not. But things were different for us. Our church required we marry from within the church. Having a pool of fewer than ten young men to choose from wasn't ideal, but it didn't matter. I had met my soulmate even though I had no idea what that word meant at the time. Our age gap was exactly that of my mom and dad, so in my mind, it was just one more sign our relationship was meant to be.

Easter came and went, and our love blossomed. While we couldn't officially date, he frequently played basketball with his brother and some friends at the local Bargersville church where I would join in. I was the only girl who played basketball with them, and as a tall girl who'd played basketball in elementary school, I was an asset to have on the court. Plus, being close to Simon certainly enticed me to be on the court even more.

Then, on the Saturday before our church's convention, Simon did something unexpected. The service had just come to an end, and Simon, in a rush to get past me, stated, "I can't talk." My heart sank. "But I love you," he quickly whispered. It was my first "I love you!" I don't remember anything else about that night other than being on the "cloud nine" I'd heard so much about.

On the following weekend, I couldn't get to the church convention quickly enough. I couldn't wait to see him and talk; it would be our first chance to speak after he told me he loved me. My family arrived in Louisville, and I sat through a service that felt like it would never end. During break, I escaped my pew to find him. There he was in a gray suit and black skinny tie to match his coal-black hair and deep brown, sultry eyes. "Hi, Simon," I said cautiously. He was surrounded by a large group of older teenagers I had never met. I felt like I'd walked into a freezer.

"Hey, Amber," he replied. "I'd like you to meet my girlfriend, Ainsel Touric."

I struggled to speak. As I gasped for breath and tried to find my words, I felt like someone had kicked me in the chest. I can't remember whether I introduced myself to Ainsel like a sane human or if I spit on her shoes, but the next thing I remember was being consoled by four adults over a hot fudge brownie sundae at Shoney's while my brother sat in utter confusion over why his sister was blowing snot bubbles because of a boy.

For the next few months, my diary was full of woe. I was shattered. What had happened in those few short days between "I love you" and the introduction of his new girlfriend? And why wasn't I notified before I was humiliated in public? I relived the situation over again and again in an attempt to figure out where I went wrong or what I'd done to deserve being treated that way.

Ginny, a friend from church who was a little older than I was, tried to console me. "I spoke to him," she said. "It wasn't anything you did or said. I heard he had to break up with you because you were 'gel bait.'"

What the hell does that even mean? As much as I tried to fit the puzzle pieces of her message together, I couldn't make sense of it. Gel bait? Bait was used for fishing. Wasn't he trying to catch me? That's what he was supposed to do, right? Get my attention? But why *gel*? *Make it make sense!* But it didn't make sense, and it was a reality I had to learn to accept.

For my fourteenth birthday, while still trying to mend my broken heart, my mom bought me a package from Glamour Shots. After all the foundation, blush, mascara, eyeshadow, and hairspray was applied, I'd transformed from a teenage girl to a young woman for my photo shoot. Of course, it was taboo for someone in our church to partake in something so worldly, so I was confused as to why my mom had made such a stand-out move, but I loved it.

When the pictures arrived, I was showing the photos to the girls seated next to me in church when the teen boys behind us started to gawk. "Let me see those," said Matthew, a boy dating a close friend of mine. Sitting next to him was a handsome young man named Brandon. And he took notice.

A few weeks later, our youth group gathered for Christmas caroling at nursing homes where our elderly church members resided. Afterward, when we reconvened in the church parking lot, we decided to go out for a late dinner. As we piled into cars, Brandon turned to me and said, "You're coming with me." And that was our first date.

Since I was fourteen, I was only allowed to go on double dates with other church friends. Usually, that consisted of going to dinner in between our church services or sitting next to each other when our youth group went out to eat. We were also allowed to spend time at one another's houses as long as parents were at home. We had a great time together, but after about a year, he chose to take a break until he was out of high school so he could enjoy his high school years. Thus, heartbreak found me once again, but this time, I had a strong feeling we would reunite. I wasn't very patient for him to come around to dating again, however. I always looked for his family at church, but he wasn't with them very often.

One summer, while Brandon was at his grandparents' farm in northern Ohio, I received a message from a church friend who was close with Brandon's family.

"Amber, Brandon's been in an accident and it's bad." The blood drained from my head, and I called her back immediately. I got all the details about what had happened, where he was in the hospital, and then began to plan to get to him.

When my parents got home, I told them about Brandon's accident. They said they'd be praying for him, but that wasn't enough for me. "What do you mean, 'you'll be praying for him'?" I demanded.

"Amber, we're not driving three hours to the hospital and three hours back in one day."

When I get my mind set on something, though, I can be pretty damn persistent. That night I stormed into my parents' room and said, "Either you can drive me there or I'll drive myself right now." We left for the hospital the next morning. As much as I tried to tell myself I'd made that trip for him, I'd made that trip for me. I'd wanted him to see how much I cared for him, but that's not what he was focused on, nor should he have been.

In the weeks that followed, he was transferred to a local hospital in Indianapolis where I visited him frequently. Every visit, I'd bring his favorite candy and his favorite flowers. But once he was discharged, I didn't see him much, and it became clear I was no longer the object of his affection. I'd done everything in my power to try to regain his attention and his love, but to no avail.

Just when I felt like all hope was gone, I began dating someone from my school during my junior year of high school. But as fate would have it, I learned he was gay. It was just as well, as neither of my parents were keen on me dating a boy who wasn't from our church. On top of that, he was Catholic, so in our church's eyes, I might as well have been dating the devil himself.

That same year, my mom chaperoned an event for my German class. I realized it was probably abnormal for a teenager to be excited for a parent to attend a class function, but I used to envy the kids in elementary school who had their parents show up and eat lunch with them. My mom and dad worked full time, so I never got to "show off" my parents. This was my chance. Plus, it felt like she was genuinely interested in something I was passionate about, which made it even more meaningful.

So, off we went to Staatskongress. Every year, students studying German gathered to participate in workshops, competitions, dancing, and displays of German language, studies, and culture. On this year, the day ended with a big dance, and the playlist consisted of lots of heavy metal music with an occasional soft rock song thrown in. As I stood against a wall, watching the head banging and everything else happening, my mother leaned over to me and said, "Get your ass off that wall. I won't let my daughter be a wallflower. Get out there and dance." I could count the number of times I'd heard my parents use profanity on one hand, so I knew she was angry.

I had no idea what she was talking about. I had been raised to believe dancing was sinful, and I'd never heard the term *wallflower* before. I envisioned big gaudy flowers that held their place on wallpaper, and I couldn't imagine how she was comparing me to something like that. But once I learned what being a wallflower meant, I knew that I was, in fact, one. It's who she raised me to be! I had always been forbidden from listening to the type of music she was now encouraging me to dance to. And because it was forbidden, I'd always had to hide anything shunned by my parents and our church, including my rock music cassette tapes and cigarettes that I hid in my 1990 Chevy Corsica hatchback. I was rebellious with boundaries: I only allowed myself to push the envelope so far. I had a "good girl" reputation to uphold, after all.

CHAPTER 3:
WILL I EVER GO HOME?

My mother was one of the most giving, nurturing women I've ever known. I'll never forget the way her hands felt as they swept across my brow when I was sick. I'll never forget the way she (sometimes in a very unhealthy way) protected her children. I'll never forget how she was the life of the party and caused spontaneous laughter at the most inappropriate times. I'll never forget how she poured love into everything she made with her hands, from the cakes she baked and decorated to the flowers she arranged for the weddings of church people, family, and friends to the everyday dinners she made for our family.

But those same soft and loving hands that nurtured me also fiercely imposed hurt, even abuse. I never knew when my mom was going to lash out. I never knew when her discontent was going to merit a month-long silent treatment. It left me second-guessing how much to reveal to her at all times, and I had to work hard to learn that love doesn't look like pain. I truly believe it was my mother's instability that has caused me to constantly scan rooms and test the energy so as to know when I need to escape danger or abandonment.

Both in church and from both sides of my family, I heard the phrase, "spare the rod, spoil the child." And it wasn't just me on the receiving end of abuse. I witnessed a close family member get chased into a closet by a parent wielding a baseball bat, and my paternal grandmother used to threaten my brother and me that she'd make us pick our own switches so she could beat us until it brought blood to our legs. It was about that time my parents stopped letting us spend much time with our paternal grandparents.

For a long time the only stories I'd heard about my mom and her childhood centered around what a clown she was. The retelling of many of her anecdotes would send the family into hysterical laughter around the Thanksgiving dinner table. She also spent an inordinate amount of time with her oldest sister who was old enough to be her mother. In fact, my mom and her niece were almost the same age and were childhood best friends. But no one ever really told me about what growing up was like for her. But I now know about some of the trauma she suffered. I've heard multiple accounts of the physical abuse she endured at the hands of her parents and the emotional abuse she and my father endured at the hands of our church family as a result of getting pregnant out of wedlock. Discovering this about my mom allowed me to better understand her actions toward me, which gave me peace. It also allowed me to see just how brave and bullheaded she was to have a child out of wedlock as a teenager.

Because I was sixteen, I was finally able to work part time without many restrictions. My newly purchased Corsica hatchback needed to be paid off. I quickly learned about debt, auto insurance, and taking care of financial responsibilities, one of which was the first 10 percent of my paycheck. Gross, not net. Tithing was not optional. "Give the first 10 percent to God," was a melody that had rung in my ears since childhood, and so much so that my first mental picture of God was a fat white guy sitting in the clouds swimming in gold coins. I remember wondering how they got the money to God. My only guess was they used a money tube like banks used to have to deliver the money straight to him.

I took a job at a large retailer new to Indiana. As a member of the toy department, I was straightening the Power Ranger figures on a shelving endcap when I saw a familiar face walking toward me. It was him. Brandon approached me and I had to remind myself to breathe. A million thoughts flew through my head. *Is this a coincidence or is he here to ask me out again?* In fact, he was.

One Sunday, soon after Brandon and I started dating again, my family drove home following the afternoon church service, something that was a diversion in our routine. Typically, we would either eat in the church basement with other families who brought their dinner, or we would go to an affordable restaurant nearby before heading back for Sunday evening service.

Six o'clock was quickly approaching, the time the service would start, but we hadn't left. Our home phone rang. It was my cousin's fiancée, and she was calling from church. My mom answered the phone. "No, we won't be back for church this evening. We actually won't be coming back to the church again at all. This afternoon was our last service there."

Hearing this, my heart dropped to my toes and I began to sob. "I will NEVER leave that church!" Pacing back and forth, my heart and body consumed with fear, I screamed until my throat hurt. "I'll find a way to go back!"

My mother shushed me, then she and my dad began explaining to my brother and me why they'd decided to permanently leave the church. The leader of our church, they explained, had been accused of child molestation, rape, and sodomy. Rumors also swirled about embezzlement and numerous affairs. The other church leaders denied knowing what had been happening in an effort to protect the minister, which was ultimately what caused my parents to make their decision.

My mom was on the phone more than usual in the weeks to come, speaking quietly so we couldn't hear. I could only assume she was talking with others who had left the church or were contemplating leaving. As for me, I was truly conflicted. What our leader had done was wrong, of course, so I understood why my parents made the decision they did. But I grew up believing only the people from our church were going to make it to Heaven. And even still, not all of them, only 144,000. I knew I had to be ultra perfect to meet Jesus face-to-face. So, this bomb, in my sixteen-year-old brain, was ripping away my chance to live eternally. And it wasn't just my soul I was worried about. The church was literally my identity. It was my only sense of normalcy and stability, the only place I really felt accepted. Without that, who was I going to be? But we never returned to that church, even after the leader was convicted of his crimes and was replaced. My parents did try to find another church to join but found it difficult. Because we came from a faith-based community with so many rules, it was hard to find a church where we could practice our faith without feeling internal conflict over ideologies and theologies.

Music had been a significant part of our worship services, and it was equally as important to us as a family. At church, we'd had a full band, a choir leader, a band leader, and a music minister who "governed" over all our churches. He'd travel to the different associated churches around the US and work with the bands and choirs. At our church, we worked on basic music, but the part I remember the most was when he instructed people how to clap on beats two and four instead of one and three. This had been a welcomed lesson, as the people clapping on the one and three beats were maddening to me. It was like fingernails on a chalkboard. Did they have zero rhythm? Nevertheless, I missed it once we were gone.

My mom and dad eventually joined a small Pentecostal Apostolic church in Greenwood, Indiana. Because I had my own car, I occasionally returned to the old church despite the fact my parents were less than thrilled. I was nervous when I first returned because I didn't know what to expect in terms of reception. But I was embraced and welcomed. There were lots of questions about how my family was doing, however, and the church never felt the same as it had.

The theological differences between the new church my parents were attending and the church we'd come from were too big for me to wrap my mind around. But for my parents and brother, after a lot of conversation, prayer, and examining the scripture through a different lens, they decided to be baptized a second time at the Apostolic church they were now calling home. Here, they were baptized in Jesus's name instead of "in the name of the Father, and of the Son, and in the Holy Spirit." As for me, I wasn't about to baptize myself into a church that wasn't going to be in the Bride of Christ, so I refused.

Still trying to appease my parents, though, I did attend their new church from time to time. It was there I received my first communion. For anyone raised Catholic or even for most Protestants, communion is a solemn event, but not frightening. That was not the case for me. I was *petrified*. The church we'd left used the scripture, "So anyone who eats this bread or drinks this cup of the Lord unworthily is guilty of sinning against the body and blood of the Lord." Thus, the only people worthy of receiving communion in their eyes were elderly "saints" of the church who had lived a nearly perfect life. Therefore, receiving communion without being perfect was essentially my removal from the Bride of Christ.

Standing in line to receive my first communion that Easter, I sobbed. I was terrified of eternal death, or worse, damnation. With each step forward, my body shook more violently, my hands trembling at the thought of tearing off a piece of bread and sealing my eternal fate. When it was my turn, I sat and took off one shoe for the foot bathing ritual. Suddenly a cool breeze flowed from the crown of my head, down my shoulders, across my back, and down to my feet. My shoulders, once nearly touching my ears, relaxed. Tears of humility and gratitude poured down my cheeks as I was whisked away to the time and place where Jesus performed this same ceremony with his disciples. It felt like an affirmation for being a true follower of Christ. All fear was gone. I took two steps forward, reached for the loaf of bread, dipped the piece I tore from the loaf in the chalice, and truly considered the gratitude due and the profundity of Easter.

Soon after rekindling my relationship with Brandon, I quit attending church with my mom, dad, and brother. Longing for the familiarity of our old church, I had to find a church that met my spiritual needs. In fact, one of the first life choices I made for myself as an adult was choosing to attend a church that had broken away from my childhood church in the 1970s, one that held the same theology.

Many of the people who had left my previous church after the leader was charged ended up going to this other church, so it was not completely foreign. Brandon's family, and most of the clique they spent time with, moved over to this church. I begged my parents to attend with me. I felt like they were being misled by false doctrine by attending the church where they had been baptized the second time. I prayed they would find their way home, but I couldn't force them.

I felt comfortable in my new church, like I was back home. There was a bit of tension between members who had been at this church for years and the flock of new people wanting to adopt this congregation as their own. It was among these "refugees" who fled the church of my childhood that I started hearing the word *cult* referenced, and frequently.

Were we really in a cult?

While I'd heard rumors ushers had started carrying guns, and that during services we weren't allowed to leave and no one was allowed to come in, no one had died. In my mind, other people were in cults, not me.

*How could **I** be brainwashed? Wasn't I stronger than that?* As it turns out, the majority of us aren't as immune to it as we'd like to think.

My dating Brandon was approved of by my family. He fit the mold as the perfect suitor my mother had in her mind: handsome, hardworking, and (most importantly!) from a family who was highly revered in the church. He also ticked all the boxes I was looking to tick at the time. And I did love him—as much as I could love anyone without fully knowing or loving myself.

I soon graduated from high school with no real clue about what I wanted to do for a career. I was accepted to Indiana State University, where my best friend from high school went and close in location to my mom's best friend. I figured I'd start out by attending general studies courses and when I made up my mind, I'd declare a major. I badly wanted to live independently of my family and to experience life on my own, but my mom informed me the only way they would pay for my college tuition was if I lived at home. My parents had saved a significant amount of money for college for both my brother and me, but when my brother got into a life-altering accident in high school, most of that money was spent on multiple trips out of state to seek extensive medical care, as it should have been.

A year passed, and my mom informed me they could no longer pay for a full four years. After the following year, I would be on my own if I wanted to continue pursuing my degree in education. So, I started working full time, going to college full time, and spending as much time with Brandon as possible in between work, studies, and school.

In my second year, I was introduced to chat rooms, a place where strangers gathered and socialized on the Internet. It was there I started talking to a man who was serving in the military at Fort Hood, Texas. I was still dating Brandon at the time, but I was so intrigued with this new man that I considered breaking it off with Brandon to pursue a new romance. Now, I'd never even met this man. We'd never exchanged photographs or even talked on the phone. But I was free to be who I was, even if it was over the Internet. I was allowed to share my dreams and not be shot down. It was a desperate plea to be seen and appreciated, but I didn't see or appreciate myself, so I had no idea this was missing in my relationship with Brandon, at least not consciously.

Brandon and my mother both convinced me I was being naive and immature and that I would be throwing away a golden opportunity. They painted every horrid picture they could imagine to make me forget my hope for this potential relationship. Brandon promised that if I walked away from our relationship, he would never return . . . even though he'd taken a break in high school to explore his freedom and come back to our relationship. I conceded—and I never spoke to the Fort Hood Internet stranger again.

CHAPTER 4:
MY MAD WEDDING PARTY

I continued going to classes and found another captivating interest (besides Internet side-pieces) while in college. As an education major, I was required to take a foreign language credit for two semesters. I opted for American Sign Language (ASL). The instructor was a hearing woman, but the two semesters with her sparked the sense of purpose I felt as a child while looking out at the two deaf members in our church's congregation. I felt a love for language again, similar to my love for the German language I'd had in high school.

I decided it was time for a new beginning. Switching career paths and schools, I began an associate's program held at the Indiana School for the Deaf. I completed two years of ASL, studying syntax and structure, as well as the culture of the Deaf community. The richness of their culture drew me in, and the complexity in the syntax of the language had me pouring over signing videos for hours. Throughout those two years, I attended Deaf church services, stayed in the dorm on campus for a couple semesters, joined a Deaf bowling league, went to Deaf football games, and attended Deaf clubs and Deaf theater. I even found I understood math for the first time ever when I took college-level algebra from a deaf instructor. The spatial aspect of the language finally made math make sense to me after struggling with it since grade 4. I wanted to dive into the deep end of Deaf culture.

As Brandon and I started spending more and more time together, my mom's actions made less and less sense to me. She constantly encouraged me to spend more time with him, but then one day called me into the bathroom as she was taking a bath and said, "Sis, I just want you to be sure that Brandon's the one for you. There are a lot of men out there. Are you sure he's the one you want to spend forever with?"

My confusion was real. This woman had been buying me bridal magazines for years. She had purchased baby clothes for my future children with Brandon to put in the hope chest Brandon had bought me. She had talked me out of breaking it off with him when I was doubting our relationship, and now this speech? So, I opted for what was easy at the moment. I stayed.

Soon after my eighteenth birthday, Brandon and I consummated our relationship, and my mom started interrogating me every time I got home. She'd go to the most controversial (and disgusting) lengths to ensure we weren't sexually active. One night, as I was in the shower following sex with Brandon, my mom stormed into the bathroom holding the underwear I'd just put in the laundry.

"You did it, didn't you?" she screamed. "You had sex with him!"

"Did you just smell my underwear? You're disgusting! No, I didn't have sex with him; we just made out!"

Back and forth we screamed at each other for twenty minutes until I finally yelled at her, "You know what, Mom? Believe what you want to believe because obviously I'm not going to change your mind."

She did later explain that her own mother had done this to her while she and my dad were dating, and while it was no excuse, I at least understood where it came from.

One year went by, then two. Then, at the Christmas following my twentieth birthday, I was absolutely sure Brandon was going to propose to me. We'd stopped at a couple jewelry cases, and I just sensed this was finally it. Then under the tree sat a giant box to me from him. I was confused. I opened it, expecting a smaller box inside. Nope. It was jumper cables. As I felt a primal scream building up in my belly, everyone laughed and laughed. I managed to contain the scream, but tears pooled in my eyes. I excused myself to freshen up so I didn't cry in front of everyone. By this time, I'd grown to hold in and hide most of my feelings.

The next box was the right size, and he knew it. My eyes were as wide as silver dollars as I cracked it open to find a white gold band with a blue topaz stone and small diamonds supporting it. "It's a promise ring," he said with a smile.

I faked my happiness. I couldn't express my true feelings without coming off as a totally spoiled child to my future husband and in-laws. But I was entirely deflated. I was never going to hear the end of my mother's endless nagging about marriage. I was sure I was a complete failure in her eyes. Soon enough, Brandon was bearing his lot of droning on from her as well. I put pressure on him. She put pressure on him. This was going to end in one of two ways: either he was going to cut and run, or he was going to cave.

More gifts of jewelry came the following Christmases, including a tennis bracelet. Finally, though, he proposed on the same night he graduated from his carpenter apprenticeship with the union. At twenty-three years old, I was at the perfect age to start having children, and at twenty-five, Brandon could say he'd waited and had not just jumped into marriage right after high school. We set the date for August 19, 2000, and wedding plans began.

Thanks to more than a decade of thumbing through bridal magazines, I knew exactly the kind of wedding I wanted. I would have a round bouquet full of white roses. My mom would bake the cake, but I wanted something understated.

My dress would be snow white with poufy shoulders and long sleeves that came to a point just below my middle finger. Lace appliqués would adorn the sleeves. We would spend our first night as husband and wife bathing in an enormous champagne glass Jacuzzi tub in the Poconos, just like the ones in the bridal magazine ads. Thankfully, someone had a candid conversation with me about what happened in those tubs, and we opted for a tropical cruise to the Caribbean in lieu of penicillin treatments.

About six months before the wedding, my mom had one of her control freak episodes. She'd been pouring over her list of wedding to-dos and the to-dos weren't getting done fast enough for her liking. The invitations hadn't yet arrived. I hadn't decided on wedding music. We hadn't completed the list for Brandon's side of wedding guests, and money was coming due for our reception site. I was feeling the pressure, and Brandon was feeling it too. Then one day, while the two of us were stressing about everything, my dad pulled us aside. "I'll give you $5,000 to fly to Hawaii and elope."

Was he serious? Because if he was serious, I was down for it. I'd do anything to escape the hell of wedding planning. Brandon was down for it too. And then it struck me: My mother would never speak to me again. I don't mean figuratively, and I don't mean she wouldn't speak to me for weeks or months. I knew she would literally never speak to me again. "Dad, I really want to take you up on that offer, but you know she won't ever speak to me again. And she might not ever speak to you again either once she finds out you offered."

My mom's—er, I mean my—wedding was just going to have to be a traditional one and done her way. To expedite plans, my mom took over the planning, and there was no stopping her. The night before the wedding, I walked into the house with one of my oldest friends, my pen pal, Steffi. Steffi and I had started writing letters through a pen pal service when I was about thirteen years old. She was from Munich, Germany. We had met once when she was a foreign exchange student in New York and took the bus to Indiana so we could spend time together. We'd stayed in touch ever since, and she had flown in to be a bridesmaid in my wedding.

As we entered the kitchen, my mom was up to her elbows in cheesecake batter, and my three-tiered wedding cake had a crumb coat of icing on it. I'd been tasked with picking out a cake topper, so Steffi and I had stopped at the only cake-decorating shop I knew and picked up the last topper they had left. It was white, but my icing was a cream-colored buttercream. I knew Mom wasn't going to be happy, but when I walked in with that white cake topper, she completely lost her shit. I burst into tears, and Steffi consoled me. The wedding rehearsal was another epic failure, and I began feeling like I was surrounded by signs this wedding wasn't supposed to happen.

Brandon and I had stopped attending church that often, so we had decided to get married at my aunt's church. Because our guest list was more than 400 people and our reception included alcohol, having the wedding at the church we attended wasn't an option anyway. Our church weddings consisted of the ceremony, cake, nuts, punch, and chocolates in the church basement, with guests sitting around watching the bride and groom opening gifts. We wanted to spare our guests the drudgery of all that and give them something they would enjoy.

My dad has always had a quiet intuition. He rarely speaks, except for when it's really important to him. As we stood outside the sanctuary of the church where I was to be married, my arm looped through his, my dad looked me dead in the eye.

"You're sure you want to go through with this?"

Something in me knew not to. I started to tear up. "There are over 400 people in there waiting for me to go through with it."

Then he gave me my final out. "And I'll go in there and tell every one of them to go home."

But I didn't say anything. I let my mom have the wedding she'd always dreamed of. My first steps toward my future husband were to a stringed quartet playing "Canon in D." The ceremony was long, and we had a wedding reception I'll remember forever. I had precisely two bites of dinner and a tiny piece of cake. But we danced, we laughed, we talked with our guests, and we cried. It was wonderful—and expensive. We had a DJ, thirteen cheesecakes and a multi-tiered wedding cake, and chocolate-covered fruit. And then there was the open bar, an option that teetered on having my parents pull the plug on paying for the entire reception. Our compromise was that we would pay for the beer and wine ourselves.

Soon enough, I was a newlywed, and my life was . . . okay. Actually, I was bored. Brandon's ideal life and my ideal life didn't align. We hadn't known we needed to have a shared vision, we'd just understood we were supposed to marry someone from the church so we'd be "equally yoked," the meaning of which I didn't fully comprehend.

We had an above-average first home. With a father-in-law who was a real estate broker and a husband who was a contractor, it was a custom-built brick house with vaulted ceilings in a quiet Midwest town. We had the picturesque Labrador retriever named Sammi, brand-new cars, and clothes from all the "right" stores. We spent weekends on our pontoon boat. We bickered about money a bit, but I heard that was to be expected in any new marriage. On the surface, we checked all the boxes and met everyone's expectations. I'd been told by many friends they wanted a marriage like the one I had with Brandon.

I soon began yearning to grow as a person, but Brandon was content. I wanted a relationship filled with meaningful conversations; I wanted to ponder the mystical side of life and explore what was possible. He found those kinds of discussions boring and would rather watch television, play golf, or work in the garden. I wanted the freedom found in owning my own business, and he wanted the perceived security found in a nine-to-five job working for someone else. I wanted a person to grow spiritually with, and he, well, didn't. Anytime I tried to dig into a deep conversation, I was met with something like "You think too much" or "Why do you overanalyze everything?" So, I would shut down, clam up, and carry on as if everything were okay.

I started attending a nondenominational Christian church a few minutes from our home. I begged Brandon to go with me, but he wasn't interested. Every weekend I'd ask him and almost every weekend I went by myself. When I'd ask him why he wouldn't attend, he'd just say he didn't feel like he needed to be in a church to have a relationship with God. He felt like spending time in nature was his church. But I craved someone with whom I could explore philosophical intrigue, and it was becoming increasingly clearer to me that the person I wanted to grow with wasn't him.

I was desperately seeking a deeper connection with someone, and I found an emotional haven in a man who was close to our family. He'd been married to a stepcousin at one time, and because he shared a daughter with her, he continued to hang around the family after they split up. He was an amazing father, and he was very sensitive and soulful. After seeing him at my family's house one day, I sought him out online. Our conversations were innocent enough, but the more he opened up to me, the more I desired him. Soon we were talking throughout the day and night. A contemplative type, I listened to his discontentment and heartbreak. And I tried to fix him.

One night after work, I came in through the garage and entered the kitchen. The light was on, but the light in the adjoining living room was off. Something felt wrong, and it made my stomach flip. Brandon was sitting next to the fireplace in the dark room, and when his eyes met mine, they pierced my soul. I knew that he knew. He stood up, went to the spare bedroom we'd converted into an office, and pulled out printed papers of the conversations I'd had with this man. I tried to lie to him, but he knew. It was all right there in black and white. I was unhappy in my marriage.

Not long after that night, the terrorist attacks on September 11 occurred. In the aftermath of the tragedy, I reflected on my life and the decisions I'd made. I felt selfish for focusing on what I didn't have, so I decided to focus on what I did have. I began by looking for the small things I was grateful for. I brought home cards and poems and other expressions of love. We spent more time with his family playing cards and games. I left love notes expressing my gratitude in his lunch, on his steering wheel, and in little places here and there. I told him how I felt about him as often as I could, but it was a Band-Aid for a marriage that never should have been.

Brandon started attending church with me, but I could tell he didn't want to be involved at the level I did. I invited the pastor over for dinner one night to learn more about the church, to explain a little about where we came from, and to see if I wanted to explore becoming a formal member. I never ended up pursuing membership, though, and eventually stopped attending because Brandon just wasn't interested and I didn't want to go by myself any longer.

In my mind, I had no option other than to try to make our marriage work. Even though I was attending other churches and starting to change my belief system bit by bit, the teachings of my childhood church still had their claws in me. The church had taught that once people married, they were never to get divorced and remarry because to do so would exclude them from making it to Heaven. Married couples had to stick it out at all costs, and if they couldn't, then they'd get divorced and remain single.

So, I stayed in my marriage, but I did quit working at the insurance company where Brandon's mom, dad, and brother also worked. Within a few months, I was hired as the scheduler for the interpreter's office at the Indiana School for the Deaf. It was there I gained a solid understanding of the code of ethics for interpreters. I was also introduced to many CODAs (Children of Deaf Adults). I listened to their life experiences, what it was like growing up with deaf parents, and the rightfully protective stances they took against inadequate interpreters.

Taking a job at a Deaf school allowed me to really use the signing skills I'd learned in college, and people took notice. In everyday conversation, I could read and sign fairly well. Others began commenting about how fast I was at finger spelling and how my syntax and facial expressions were accurate. It was when I found myself taking actual interpreting jobs that I froze, however. The fear of not being perfect, a fear ingrained in me from childhood, was palpable.

My fear was evident on the day I was sitting in the president's office of the Deaf school, as all other interpreters were out on other jobs and I was the only option left. Twelve sets of eyeballs were on me, relying on me for communication. Beads of sweat formed on my scalp and slowly started to make their way to the front of my hairline and down my neck. Within fifteen minutes, I was soaked. The superintendent, who had been angry about interpreters not being available, showed compassion for me and asked the meeting participants to reschedule for another date and time. Strike one.

After that experience, I knew I needed to hone my skills and build my confidence, so I began taking small thirty-minute to hour-long interpreting jobs at a local nonprofit. Around the time I started feeling okay about the work I was doing there, I got an urgent call.

"Amber, we've tried everyone. Can you please interpret for President Jimmy Carter at his Habitat for Humanity event in Indianapolis?"

Oh, for god's sake. Are you freaking kidding me? I then thought to myself, *Well, there's no time like the present to see just how far you've come.*

I didn't know if I would be on camera, but I did know that if there was the slightest chance I'd be meeting a former president of the United States, I would be wearing my best. I donned a long black velour skirt, black tights, and a white Angora sweater . . . for a heated arena.

Like a repeating nightmare, a steady trickle on my scalp grew to an all-consuming fire hose of sweat that drenched my hair. My Angora sweater was literally sticking to my body. And in front of a former president. I was completely humiliated and defeated. That was strike two. There would be no strike three. I worked at the school for only a few more months.

During one of my last weeks at the school, I heard a thunderous roar coming from the auditorium, just steps away from my office. It was extremely rare to hear much of anything in the school unless you were in the cafeteria, so I rushed to the auditorium to see what was going on. I saw a young man on the stage drawing on a massive canvas, booming music playing as he worked. It was incredibly moving, but I didn't know why. The vibration of the music sent chills down my spine, and the picture on the canvas transformed into a lighthouse on an ocean shore. Lights out, music up, and from that lighthouse, a stream of yellow light poured out onto the crowd. The beacon of light circled by our eyes again and again and again. The air left the auditorium.

I'd caught only the tail end of this speaker's presentation, but I was inspired so much I immediately went home to learn more about the company he'd mentioned. I didn't know a lot, but I could feel I was supposed to work for them. I didn't think the company would be local, and I knew Brandon would never consider moving, but I hopped online anyway to find out as much as I could.

I couldn't believe it. They were a local speaking group . . . in Indianapolis! My heart started beating faster. They were hiring a full-time administrative professional, so I discussed the opportunity with Brandon. He had concerns, of course. "What about ASL? You're almost done. Don't you just have a gym class left to get your degree?"

I did. He was right. But it was clear that any kind of career as an interpreter wasn't the right fit for me. And if I were to switch to speech therapy or social work, it would mean another four years of schooling. So, we agreed I would apply, and if I got the interview, we'd wait and see what happened.

I got the interview. When I arrived, I was greeted by a tall blond guy, definitely not the one I saw on stage at the Deaf school. This man was closer to my age.

"You here for the job?" he asked.

"I am," I said nervously.

"Sure you don't want to reconsider?" he said with a laugh. "I'm just kiddin'. Come on back." He escorted me back to the office where his wife, Polina, the VP of the company, worked.

It turned out to be the least formal interview I'd ever taken part in. Polina and I discussed my experience and skills, as well as the pay rate. As I listened to her speak in very clear English, I couldn't help but think to myself, *I hear an accent, but it's not like anything I've ever heard before.*

In her office were three clocks: one set for Moscow, one for Melbourne, and one for Chicago. "What's the clock situation?" I asked.

Polina explained she had been born in Moscow to Russian parents. They moved to Melbourne when she was a young girl, then she moved to Chicago to attend college.

"I also traveled to Israel where I backpacked across the country," she went on to state.

Who was this woman? I'd never met anyone like her. I was curious to get to know her more. The pictures she had in her office of Mary and Jesus seemed to be Catholic in nature, but the way she spoke about her beliefs seemed quite Protestant. My mind reeled, and I was excited for what the future might bring.

I got the job and started on December 4, 2001. It was just a day after my birthday, and it was the best gift I could've given myself. In the beginning, I did a lot of grunt work: running to get stamps, scheduling UPS pickups, ordering shipping supplies, and filtering emails to send to Polina. Three of us—a special effects and video editor, Polina, and I—shared a small office, so we got to know one another very well. Within just weeks of taking the job, I got a call that a great-aunt had passed on my mother's side. Without batting an eye, Polina offered me time off. Just months later, in 2002, my maternal grandmother passed away. More time off. I was so grateful.

Polina and I talked about everything: my childhood, the church I was raised in, losing close family at an early age, and having so much loss since then. She was intrigued by my big family. She'd moved to the States with just her mother and father. She had no siblings, and the entire time I'd known her, I'd only met one extended family member over a Christmas holiday. Through our conversations and her observations about my family and life, it didn't take long for her to look me straight in the eye and say, "You know, you probably ought to write a book."

On the home front, Brandon and I decided to sell our newlywed home, move closer to the city, and downsize our mortgage by purchasing an older but well-cared-for home. Brandon was starting to spend more and more time around my new bosses, Polina and her husband, Ben. We spent most of our time together at their home.

Our company represented three speakers, with Ben being the original one. He was an ordained minister, but he wasn't an acting minister at any one church. Growing up as a self-declared Easter and Christmas Catholic, he practiced his faith as a nondenominational Protestant. He and the other two speakers traveled around the US doing school, church, and even corporate keynote speaking events.

After a few months of working, I'd mastered the tasks of the job I was initially taught. I was spending more time twiddling my thumbs than I was helping with the business, so I asked Polina whether there was anything else I could be doing, and she happily broke out the speaker binders full of green and white paper. She walked me through the anatomy of each speaking gig in the binder and I happily learned all about the speaking side of the company. While I truly enjoyed my job at the Deaf school, this was the first job I truly took great pride in, and it showed. Polina frequently left thank you notes on my computer screen sharing what good work I was doing.

Over the next couple months, I took over organizing the speaking gigs. Once I felt at home, and I knew that Polina understood my character and my intent, I also began making suggestions for the business. With no ego at all, Polina always replied, "Let's try it!"

Then, as I was sipping my morning coffee one morning, Polina slipped into my office. We had moved into a more formal workspace by this time on the Old Northside of Indianapolis. "We're thinking about hiring a marketing director," she said.

I asked her if she had anyone in mind, then with a deep breath said, "What if I took the position?"

"You've done a great job so far, but do you know anything about marketing?"

"I don't, but I'm willing to learn."

"Let me talk it over with Ben and we'll let you know."

Not too long after, they agreed the job was mine. They didn't have to take on another salary, and I kept my old duties plus my new ones. They hired a marketing consultant to help me learn everything relevant. Work life was looking bright.

CHAPTER 5 :
REFLECTIONS THROUGH
THE LOOKING GLASS

In taking on my new job title, I started experiencing impostor syndrome, so I decided to go back to school to finish my degree. And it was during my time at Indiana Wesleyan University (IWU), where I received my bachelor's degree in business, that I had two revelatory spiritual awakenings.

The first occurred when I took a course based on the teachings of Paul/Saul. In my childhood church we had been taught how to interpret the scriptures through sermons and Sunday School lessons. As a college student, I saw these scriptures in a new light. I now looked at them through my own perspective, and I raged. How could such a jerk merit the space of nearly half of the New Testament books of the Bible? I prattled on and on to my parents one weekend about what a misogynist Paul the Apostle of Jesus was. Throughout it all, my dad cast that same sly smirk toward my mother as if to say, "We've got our hands full with this one."

Before I knew it, my college years were coming to an end. During my last semester at IWU, our academic advisers met with us to let us know if there were any classes we were missing prior to graduation. I was missing one elective. I could choose to test out of Intro to Business Ethics or Intro to World Religions. I knew ethics. But since I only ever had access to Christianity because I was kept from entering anything other than a Protestant church, I was curious to learn about other religious beliefs.

After completing all my other courses, I received a study guide for the Intro to World Religions test and made my own flashcards to prepare for it. I studied as much as I could before my eyes crossed, then called my mom over to help me. I fully expected her to bash the beliefs of the other religions as we studied, but surprisingly, she didn't, and therefore, I felt like it might be safe to share with her that I was having serious doubts about my faith and what I'd been taught. I was dying to tell her how I was feeling, and it welled up in my belly until there was no other option—I verbally vomited all over her. I just couldn't keep it to myself any longer.

"Mom, I have something to share with you, but you can't be mad at me." Her eyes pierced a hole through my soul. *Maybe things would be different, and we could talk like adults since I was married.* That was my hope.

"What is it?"

"Promise you won't get mad at me."

"I can't promise you that. I don't know what you're about to tell me."

"I don't really identify as a Christian anymore."

She wasn't just mad, she was **seething** mad. And so began her silent treatment. She didn't speak to me for weeks. I tried calling her, but it would go to voicemail. I called my dad to talk to him.

"She just needs some time, Sis."

I'm sure he wasn't thrilled about this either, but at least he didn't abandon me until I conformed to his will. Instead of viewing my admission as a brave move—me seeking answers for myself—my mom viewed it as a personal attack. I couldn't take the silence any longer. I called her, apologized on her voicemail, and asked for a call back.

"I don't want you to do this just for me, Amber."

If I wanted a relationship with her, my only option was to surrender and continue my Christian duty by going to church, singing worship songs, participating in church activities, and praying for all the sinners of the world. And so, I did.

It was just as well, I supposed. I worked for a Christian organization, and it wouldn't make sense to be employed by a Christian-based organization as a heathen. I dug in deep at work and soaked up the new marketing opportunity. I sought out more high-paying corporate events, and Ben and Polina worked to land one of the most prestigious speaking engagements in the world, which, when landed, officially gave Ben the title "International Keynote Speaker."

That year, Brandon and I traveled with Ben and Polina to Cabo San Lucas where we had a memorable trip, but on the way back to our room on the last night, Ben and Polina got to hear firsthand just how little Brandon believed in me and in my dreams.

When we'd gotten married, Brandon had bailed me out of thousands of dollars in credit card debt from failed multilevel marketing aspirations. He was the breadwinner by a long shot. Through our married years, we had more than one conversation about how multi-passionate I was and that I had to choose one thing to focus on or I was going to fail at everything.

On the walk back to our hotel rooms that night, I was on a high from a great vacation. "I want to play piano," I said out of the blue. Both of my aunts played piano, as did my paternal grandmother. It was a family legacy, and I could feel the magic begging to be expressed. "I feel like an artist without a brush, and I think the piano might be my brush," I admitted as we walked down the dark Cabo streets.

Brandon's voice, louder than normal, came bellowing my way after I expressed my newfound desire. "Oh, you mean like how you wanted to sell $10,000 in makeup? Or how you wanted to learn to play drums? Oh, how about when you were going to get your degree in education, or that time you changed your degree to ASL? You never finish anything you start. Why would we waste our money on piano lessons when you're going to take lessons for a few months and then stop?"

Time stood still. I didn't know how to respond. He wasn't wrong, but I felt really beat up on. He'd spoken to me like this in private before, but this was the first time we had witnesses. Apparently, the alcohol made him bolder than normal.

"Do you both hear this? This is the encouragement I get when I want to go after my dreams. I hear this shit all the time." I saw the looks of concern from Ben and Polina. Soon after we returned from the trip, Ben and Polina asked us to their house with the offer to counsel us, but Brandon didn't want anyone else involved in our marriage.

It was clear Brandon held resentment toward me for all he'd done to help me recover financially. The arguments about money were becoming more frequent, and I started nit-picking about the spending decisions he was making instead of owning my own mistakes.

The nail in the coffin for our marriage took place during one final trip together to the Bahamas. In full transparency, I was finished with the marriage by that time and should have told Brandon not to come, but I felt like I was in a constant state of push–pull. *Do I hurt him now to save him later, or appease him now so I spare him the pain in the moment?* But I selfishly didn't want to miss the trip, as the young man I was interested in was on the island. Heinous, I know. I have no excuses.

The day after we arrived, my mother called. The fees to call the Bahamas at the time were astronomical, so I knew she'd gotten word of our impending divorce or she wouldn't have made the call. I'm intuitive and an empath, and I could feel her energy on the other end of the line. As I was handed the phone, I was primed for a fight.

"Amber, what's wrong? The Lord woke me from a dream I was having. You and Brandon were in a boat and the boat was sinking. I know something's wrong. What's going on?"

"Who called and told you, Mom?" I said, annoyed as ever.

She denied culpability over and over again until I broke her down and she admitted it was Brandon who had called in a last-ditch attempt to "save our marriage." Any shred of hope remaining was shattered in that one moment.

After five years married, and a total of twelve years together, the end had come. I was being manipulated by my mother and by Brandon—and I'd had enough. I wanted out of the

controlling grasp that had dominated me for my entire life.
I was done.

Just before the divorce was final, my mind was on everything
but work. Things started slipping through the cracks. I missed
booking a flight for a gig for our speaker in Florida, and my
wandering mind was impacting the bottom line of Ben and
Polina's business. As a result, I was fired from my dream
job. While I completely understood, and in all honesty, was
surprised it hadn't happened sooner, I was devastated just
the same.

Meanwhile, my parents weren't supportive of our decision
to divorce. In fact, it wasn't until Brandon called while I was
staying with them during the end of our separation that
they started to understand it truly wasn't going to work out.
The abuse I endured during that phone call sent me into a
spiral, and I tried to take my life. I wanted to die, and I knew
if I stayed in that marriage, I'd be successful. Soon after, my
parents scheduled a moving truck and moved me out of our
marital home while Brandon was at work because it was clear
he wasn't going to let me go easily.

Back in my childhood home, I was hired and then fired
within sixty days from a home health agency. Soon after losing
that job, I began working for an apartment community as a

leasing agent. I commuted over an hour to get to work at a time when gas was more than four dollars a gallon, and it didn't take a rocket scientist to realize that on a wage of twelve dollars an hour, it wasn't sustainable. To save money, I began lying to my parents about staying at a friend's house when I was actually sleeping in the community center of the apartment complex I worked for. Brandon found out and threatened to call the police on me, so I started just sleeping in my car. Eventually, I had to leave that job, as the economy wouldn't allow me to continue living as I was. I filed for bankruptcy, surrendered my car, bought the cheapest used car I could find, took a job as a waitress, and moved back to my parents' home.

It was a lonely time, and I wanted to start dating again. Truth be told, I didn't want to be divorced, I just didn't want to be married to Brandon. So, I typed into the Yahoo search engine: "How to make sure I never end up with the wrong partner again." (It never occurred to me I might hold the answers within myself!) I found an article that told me to write out everything missing from my marriage but in a way that delivered it from the perspective of what I wanted in my next marriage or relationship.

So I created a list of everything I wanted in a partner. I kept this list in a file folder, and I read it every day for the next month. Then, as the years went on, I revisited the list regularly and felt reinvigorated and hopeful that *he* was out there somewhere. I still have that list somewhere in storage, but it looked something like this:

- *I want a man who desires deep conversations with me.*
- *I want a man who is spiritually active and involved in our home.*
- *I want a man who wants to grow together and explore who and what we can become.*
- *I want a man who embraces all of the possibilities brought about by "unconventional work."*
- *I want a man who loves to read.*
- *I want a man who will explore the what-ifs.*

And so it continued for an entire page and a half.

Brandon continued to call and email me for nearly two years. I changed my number twice due to his excessive calls, but because I felt guilty about leaving him, I'd end up giving him the new number. During one of these calls, I shared my list with him, to which he responded, "So . . . what? You're keeping a grocery list of what you want in a man? Good luck, Amber. No one's perfect. You'll never make it without me."

His words got to me. Was I being unreasonable? No matter. I kept this list with me for the first few years after the divorce and read it at least once a week. I didn't know it at the time, but I was starting a practice that would teach me exactly how to manifest my ideal man.

CHAPTER 6 :
CURIOUSER

Tenneva, the same cousin and best friend who I tried on frilly dress after frilly dress with, was given the option of whether to attend church as a teenager. She started showing up to church less and less, and we grew apart in our teenage years. She was off living life, while I was consumed with church... until shortly before my divorce when our childhood friendship was reignited and we began to share many memorable adventures together. The first excursion we opted for was a trip to the Bahamas. I made an utter fool of myself on that trip, but I also had a copious amount of fun. We both did.

Tenneva and I made multiple trips back to the Bahamas over the next couple years. Memories were made, as were friendships I still cherish to this day. My first relationship after my divorce was a long-distance one with another man from the Bahamas. I flew back and forth for about a year and a half, and he flew to Indiana once. I spent thousands of dollars on trips, rental cars, gifts, and food. I bought his ticket to Indiana for my thirtieth birthday, and he spent about sixty dollars on my birthday sushi dinner. And when he told me he cheated on me, I forgave him because, as he said, his heart belonged to me but his body was free game to other women. So, I stayed. I felt like I hadn't given my all to my marriage, and I wanted to be able to say that I'd given this relationship everything.

Toward the end of that relationship, I received an invitation from Tenneva to attend a self-improvement conference. It changed the way I saw life and how I saw myself. During this two-and-a-half-day event, I was introduced to strange new words I'd had never heard in that context before like *manifesting* and *intention*. Up until that point, I had viewed life as a series of events, good and bad, that were happening to me without my control. I was conditioned to use prayers when things didn't go right in my life and to thank God for blessing me when things went well. God was in control. I had been taught to rely on an outside source to get me through life's ups and downs, and although it provided me some source of comfort and normalcy, it kept me from being who I truly wanted to be. I was a victim or a recipient of happenstance rather than a captain of my own ship. At this conference, however, I heard someone tell me for the first time that I could create my own life and steer to the shores of my choosing.

During those days I spent at this personal development seminar, a couple of events stood out to me, but one event in particular shook me to my core: the locked door lunch fiasco. As we broke for a late lunch one day, the facilitator said, "This break will be thirty minutes. It's 3:30 now. Be back by 4:00. If you're not back by 4:00, the doors will be locked and you will not be able to get back in."

I felt like this was my first chance to prove to myself I could produce the life I wanted, so I made up my mind to be safely behind the doors once the clock struck four. I ran across the street to a deli. As I stood in line to order my meal, I pondered whether I had time to eat in the deli or take the food to the parking lot. After about five minutes of waiting in line, I decided I could eat quickly enough to get back in time. With every bite I took, I looked at my watch and calculated when I'd need to leave. I scarfed down my food and whipped back into the parking lot with three minutes to spare. I arrived at the door at 3:59 and pulled on the handle. Locked. I ran around to the windows outside of the room where I saw almost every other student.

But I made it back before 4:00! I thought to myself as a lump formed in my throat. My whole body tensed up.

Unbeknownst to me, the group facilitator had locked the doors before 4:00 on purpose. He had a point to prove, but what? My mind began to focus on all my failures. *You can't do anything right.*

Just before we'd left on break, not coincidentally, we'd been led in a discussion regarding the concept of manifesting and how we are, in fact, cocreators of everything that happens in our lives. As most people do when first introduced to this concept, I went through my bag-o-traumas and thought of every conceivable reason why and how I was **not** a creator of the life I'd been living.

And now, there I stood at the weighty, solid double doors of my classroom, trying to get them to budge. As I stood there, I began to make excuses as sweat rolled down my scalp. And then, a flashback: "You create the life you live." At that very moment, I asked myself a question that would guide me through every difficulty I would encounter thereafter.

"What could you have done differently to produce a more desirable result?"

Just then, a sliver of light came pouring through the double doors. Through the crack, the facilitator said, "You're late, but come in and take your seat."

I felt a range of emotions. I felt embarrassed I wasn't on the side of the door I'd imagined, as well as a sense of relief I could continue participating and learning. It was at this moment I realized my life wasn't a culmination of good and bad things that happened to me; instead, I realized that as a cocreator of my own life, it was my responsibility to do things for me and to do them on purpose.

When I completed the conference, my mom and dad hesitantly attended my "graduation" from the eye-opening event. It all sounded a little too "new age" to them, but in a show of solidarity, they attended. I then took one more trip back to the Bahamas to end my relationship. I hadn't just given this relationship my all, I had given it too much. No woman who knows how to love herself negotiates what she wants, needs, and deserves in a relationship.

Mom and Dad changed churches again and landed at an Assemblies of God church. I went with them a few times and recognized it as the same church where I'd rededicated my life to God for the fourth or fifth time just about a year prior. I knew that to maintain a relationship with my parents I had to shift back to their beliefs, so I decided to once again attend church with them.

As time moved on, I got more involved in the church. I volunteered to pray for prayer requests submitted by church members once a week. I joined the choir for the annual Singing Christmas Tree and Independence Day events. I joined my mom in the kitchen from time to time for occasions when she was in charge of the kitchen. I became the daughter she'd always wanted.

Less than a year later, my mother began experiencing abdominal pain. She underwent a partial hysterectomy, and her body just didn't heal. More tests showed spots on her pancreas. It was cancer. She was immediately scheduled for a procedure that would tell if the cancer had metastasized. As we entered the hospital waiting room, the doctor approached.

"I want you to understand what to expect. The Whipple procedure can take as long as twelve hours, but if we get in there and see that the cancer has metastasized, we will sew her back up. If you are called to a quiet room and we've been in surgery for less than three hours, I want you to understand it is very probable we don't have good news."

Less than two hours later, we watched the surgeon walk toward us. The weight of a hundred elephants sat on my shoulders. I couldn't cry. I couldn't speak. I couldn't move. I just sat in a daze, waiting with fifteen other family members to hear the finality of the doctor's words.

"The cancer has spread to her liver and other vital organs. It's stage four. We can refer her out to an oncologist who can set up treatments, but the reality is that there is a very low five-year survival rate for stage four pancreatic cancer. I would say she has three to six months to live."

One by one, heavy hearts retreated from that quiet room until it was just my dad and me. I finally found the courage to catch his gaze. He looked straight into my eyes.

"How do I tell her when she wakes up? How do you tell someone they have months left to live? It's not supposed to happen like this. I'm going to be that man eating alone at the diner that everyone pities." Grief had already consumed him.

I, on the other hand, hopped right over grief and pointed my compass straight toward denial. I researched every natural and alternative method to cure pancreatic cancer. No one was going to tell me there was no hope. I stayed online for forty-eight hours straight, looking for something we could do. In desperation, we drove her to the Chicago area for treatment and flew her to New York. She was a trooper.

I didn't consider what the doctor said as being true until Mom got back from her trip to New York. As she sat on my aunt's couch, I decided to massage her feet to help bring her pained body some comfort. Then, when I touched her foot, the tears flowed from me like a river.

"Finally!" she said. "I was starting to think you weren't going to miss me at all when I'm gone."

The one thing Mom brought to almost every conversation was her sense of humor. We laughed, and after a consoling hug for both of us, I made up my mind. Although my belief in God was waning, I chose to be the daughter she needed me to be so she could pass away in peace. I moved back into my childhood home to help be a caretaker for her. I took a part-time job at a company known for carrying organic produce (to get a discount on Mom's alternative medicine foods and supplements). Additionally, I arranged a fundraiser for her and raised about $30,000 for her alternative and complimentary medical treatments. During this time, I also took a contract role at an urban charter school to recruit students to supplement my income.

I prayed with her regularly. We kept Southern Gospel playing on the television and radio. We went to church together when she felt like it. We inundated her with trinkets engraved with Jeremiah 29:11: "For I know the plans I have for you," declares the LORD. "Plans to prosper you and not to harm you, plans to give you hope and a future." We showered her with love.

Then, one night, as I walked into our home with my hair plaited down both sides of my head, she slowly turned her head from the hospital bed we'd positioned in our living room.

"Hi, Sis! I've always loved your hair like that. I sure do love you."

And those were the last words I'd ever hear from her. The next day, on May 23, 2008, my mom waited for her one true love to wake up and give her a final kiss. She then took her last breath and passed away at fifty years old. In typical Mom fashion, she went out with a bang. It was the Friday before Memorial Day weekend, so those out of work and school all made their way to her wake and funeral the following Tuesday.

After the funeral, calls and visits slowed down. The house became eerily quiet. I vowed to stay in the house with Dad until he was ready for me to move out. My dad's extracurricular activities included church services, grief classes at church, and time spent at my mom's grave talking to her. I found myself completely alone—truly alone for the first time in my life. And it was terrifying. There was no one to tell me who I had to be anymore. There was no one to take care of except myself, but I didn't have a clue what that would even look like. I'd either been abused by others or myself my entire life.

A few months after my mom passed, my dad started dating again. He couldn't bear staying in the same home where we'd all lived and where she'd died. I was forced to find a new place to live. A dear friend of mine was also seeking a place, as her lease was up at her apartment complex. We had met about a year prior when we worked at an airport rental car company. She was timid with me at first, something I recognized because it has always taken time for me to trust others as well. But over time we'd become close.

Even though I'd been fired by Polina and Ben, I'd remained in touch with them. Polina had one-half of a duplex in Indianapolis that was vacant and in pretty rough shape. She offered my friend and me the space to rent at a rate that was more than reasonable. Before we moved in, we bought some paint for the walls. We hand-sanded the wood floors and gave them a coat of polyurethane. We deep cleaned everything from the basement to the second floor, and within a couple of weeks, we called the place home. It was a labor of self-love and love for one another.

As for self-care, I began to exercise. I walked a path a few blocks north of our duplex to a beautiful Catholic church. Every time I saw the church, I felt it pulling me to come in, sit, and pray, but I didn't. Not then. I'd only been to two Catholic churches in my life: my first in 2003 when I went to Munich, Germany, to visit my friend and grade school pen pal, Steffi, and the second when I attended one with Brandon. We just so happened to go during a Mass done in Spanish, so I didn't understand any of it, and I was too intimidated by the rituals I didn't know, so I decided to forgo my curiosity.

The energy of the time and space at this time in my life felt very familiar, almost like being baptized in Deaf culture again. I knew I was supposed to be learning something. I was living with a Black woman and her son and working in a predominantly Black charter school in Indianapolis. When school began, I was petrified I was going to do or say something wrong or offensive, so my plan was to keep my mouth shut and observe.

At the school, my role shifted from one in marketing to a teaching one in their technology lab. One of my duties was to check students into breakfast in the morning. I worked with a food worker, Tanisha. She was a character. Hilarious, but hard. I could tell I had one shot to make an impression on her, and if I ruined it, I wouldn't get another. My plan to observe was in full effect.

"Pshhh . . . Here she come with her bougie ass tryin' to act like she got it like that."

She made me laugh, not because I knew what she was talking about, but because of the energy she had. I knew the energy, and I knew she was pulling precisely zero punches. I'd never been around anyone that direct before. So, I kept my mouth shut, smiled, and nodded. In my mind, I was making notes about times she would use words I hadn't heard before. My hope was to try to wrap my mind around them conceptually.

Time passed, and I started to really love the people I was working with. I learned that Tanisha wasn't so much hard as she was just expecting people to be direct, not false. And as a person who doesn't do well understanding subtle language, I admired and respected that about her. I also learned so much about the kids and the hardships many of them faced. I got to know the teachers, to laugh with them, cry with them, party with them, and learn from them. I was invited to house parties and went to predominantly Black nightclubs.

One of my coworkers came to nickname me White Chocolate. "You cool," she'd say. "You don't try to talk Black or wear your hair in cornrows. You're just you."

Working there was the most eye-opening two years of my life. I can only equate it to what it must be like to live in a different country and learn the different cultures, languages, and spice palettes of a nation. It was a life-changing experience in all the best ways.

My life was so different with my mom gone. She had been such a strong presence that it now felt like I was free for the first time ever. On some days I wished I could pick up the phone and call her, and on others, I mindlessly enjoyed not being under the thumb of her constant judgment and control. I felt like her death made space for my growth. In a world that deifies the dead, it's a risk to be that honest without the fear of being judged.

During a particularly difficult time after my mom's death, I reached out to a friend who I'd met through my time working at the Deaf school to seek solace. She told me something I'd never even considered. "She's not gone, Amber. Do you know what we are at our most basic state?"

"Um . . . cells? Atoms?" I replied.

"No. At our most basic state, we're all comprised of energy. And the first law of thermodynamics states *the total energy in a system remains constant, although it may be converted from one form to another*. Essentially, we, in our broken-down state, are energy. And since it can't be created or destroyed, neither can we. We always have been and we always will be."

I hung up and sat there with my mind reeling. Surely I'd been taught about this in science class, but I'd also been taught to ignore much of science class because they taught topics like evolution and the big bang theory, both of which, I was taught, went against creationism.

How had I missed out on a topic of such significance? My life shifted at that moment. I shared what I learned with my roommate. In the past I'd heard her refer to a book she said she read every year, *Conversations with God: An Uncommon Dialogue*. She'd mentioned she didn't think I was ready for it yet. When I told her about this revelation, though, she said, "This is a fiction book, Amber. You might read concepts that contradict how you grew up believing. If it doesn't feel right, just keep reading. Take what feels right and leave what doesn't."

I rarely took book recommendations at the time, but I took that one, and I've taken plenty since then due to the impact this particular book had on me. It opened my eyes to a new way of thinking and living. I knew there was more to God than what I'd been told, and I had to learn more.

As I was exploring a whole new world, my dad was about to start a new life of his own. The woman he'd begun dating only months after mom died agreed to marry him. He did share with me right before they were married, however, that there was a chance it might not work out. His fiancée seemed to have some insecurities about my mom, which I didn't understand. Competing with a dead woman just didn't make sense, in my mind. But they proceeded to marry anyway, and I intentionally tried not to speak about my mom when in her presence so as to not trigger her for my dad's sake.

I also started dating again. I dated a number of men, enjoyed a "situationship," and had a blast with a friend with benefits, but making a commitment was never really an option with anyone. Frustrated, I became down on myself and my ability to find a long-lasting and fulfilling relationship. So, I joined a website specifically to find a Christian man. Surely here I would find a high-caliber man with strong morals. After a few weeks, I found a man with a photo that was blurry but easy enough to make out. I could tell it was at least a few years old based on the background, but he appeared to be handsome.

I invited him to fly from New York to visit me in Indianapolis. I felt comfortable enough to have him stay at our home since my roommate would be there. But a couple days before his arrival, my roommate found a way to attend her best friend's wedding in another state. Because I'm a people pleaser, I felt uneasy about asking this man to get his own place, so I decided it would be fine, even though my roommate questioned whether it was a good idea. Stubborn as ever, I didn't want to inconvenience him by asking him to find a hotel room.

When my roommate returned home after her trip, she found me sitting on our couch with my then-stepsister consoling me as I drank spiced rum straight from a large bottle. I had bruises all over my body, teeth marks on my neck and arms, a bruised cheek, and all the evidence I needed to put him away. But I couldn't do it. I couldn't face him again after what had happened.

After this assault, I began recognizing a pattern of self-sabotage, and I knew I needed to seek out professional help. Through therapy, I discovered that I felt I deserved payback due to the hurt I put my ex-husband through when I asked him for a divorce. Logically, I knew no one deserved to go through emotional or physical abuse, rape, disrespect, or infidelity, but I wasn't everyone else. I viewed my fate as karma.

I chose to remain single for more than a year. Once I was ready, I began to date more intentionally. I didn't always choose perfectly, but at least I was purposely choosing with my own happiness and sense of self in mind. Although I didn't find my soulmate, I did notice I was attracting men who were more aligned with what I was looking for. I dated men who were open to commitment and spirituality and saw the world through a different lens than I was used to. Some men were absolutely perfect for me, but I met them at the wrong time or we simply didn't have chemistry, but each of them helped me see myself differently. I felt more valued because I finally started to feel seen for me. They allowed me space to grow into the woman I wanted to be for the husband I was certain I would one day meet.

I widened my dating options and joined a well-known dating site where I met an Indian man who caught my eye. He was a doctor of pharmacology and we enjoyed stimulating intellectual conversations. I'll never forget the first time I went on a date with him. We were touring the Indianapolis Art Museum, checking out the different cultures represented there. I was eager to share how I grew up and how my beliefs had evolved since leaving the cult-like church I was raised in.

"Well, in Hinduism, it's fairly common to see every Christian denomination as a cult."

While I was stunned by his directness at first, we had an enlightening conversation about the worldview of Christianity and its brutal history, a history I must have missed in my textbooks. It was a conversation that would have at one time caused me to lash out, but I didn't. Again, my consciousness expanded to consider a worldview other than my own.

Meanwhile, my roommate had become more like a sister to me than a friend. I'd share new epiphanies and studies with her, and I clearly remember her saying, "How did this white girl from Bargersville, Indiana, turn out to be Amber Powers?" And the answer? It was by keeping my mouth shut when it was my turn to learn, and it was by keeping my mind open enough to learn . . . to question what I'd been taught growing up.

After that conversation, I had a flashback to a Bible study I'd participated in with my dad as a teenager. When the study was over, he said, "Sis, there's a verse in the Bible in Second Timothy that says to 'Study to show yourself approved.' So many people try to argue their point to be the correct perspective, but it is my opinion that you should work your hardest to disprove your opinions and interpretations so that what is left standing is solid. What's left is the truth."

My dad was right. I learned that a function of the ego is protection. Thus, the fear of being wrong is the caution tape that keeps us from crossing the bridge and making connections with others who are different from us, others who believe differently than we do and may even keep us from personally evolving.

More conversations with my dad continued to return to me. When I was a teenager, he had an epiphany about a particular scripture, and it was almost as though he had found the key to life. It was like he had figured out an understanding of something he had been missing. I don't know whether he had been watching prayers go unanswered or what was happening at the time to make him ponder this, but I do remember specifically how excited he was about coming to a new understanding of Mark 11:24. "Therefore I tell you, whatever you ask in prayer, believe that you have received it, and it will be yours."

"We've been doing it all wrong!" I remember him saying.

"Doing what wrong?" I asked.

"Praying. The Bible says that we have to believe we have received it *before* we receive it. That's the key!"

Reflecting on this memory reminded me about that list I wrote post-divorce, and I took that principle to heart.

While I continued going to my mom and dad's church for a while after my mom passed, I seriously contemplated converting to Catholicism throughout 2010 to 2012. I craved stillness and silence as opposed to loud music and entertainment-like worship services. I simply wanted to be quiet—to have quiet surround me—so I could hear what God wanted for me. I was tired of being told what to believe.

It was during this time of contemplation that I also started a new job at a timeshare exchange company in Indianapolis. I was required to attend a new software release training, and as class was about to begin, the finest man I have ever seen in my entire life walked in. His skin was brown with flecks of gold that made him shimmer like an angel. He wore a crisp navy blue suit with a gray pinstripe fedora.

"Amber, don't stare. He'll think you're a creep," I told myself. I glanced his way occasionally, then saw him searching for something.

"I forgot my pen," he said. "Does anyone have one?"

Here's my chance! I dove headfirst into my purse on the hunt for the first writing instrument I could find. I reached his table, handed him the pen, and told him I'd see him after class to get it back. At the end of the training when I approached him to retrieve my pen, he said something really quippy and funny, but I was too shy to respond. Later, I asked some coworkers his name and whether he was dating someone.

"His name is Dee, but I'm not sure what his deal is."

Over the next while, I frequently saw Dee on the sales floor at work, but he always seemed to have a thin, redheaded coworker by his side. Convinced he was in a relationship,

I opted to simply focus on my work, which was just as well since I was at the tail end of a long-distance relationship (or so I thought) with a lawyer who lived in Chicago. He was a very faithful Catholic, something that had intrigued me most about him. During our "courtship," he was the first to really introduce me to the mysteries of the faith. I later found out he was engaged the entire time we were together, and he had a child. But he'd sparked an interest in this mystical Christian faith, and I knew although our time was finished, I needed to follow my interest in Catholicism.

CHAPTER 7:
BEHIND THE VEIL

A good friend of mine was a practicing Catholic. I'd confided in her that I was drawn to the church and I had attended a few services, but they'd felt too commercial and way too White. I didn't want to be around more people like me. I wanted to learn and be surrounded by diversity. I yearned to be in a traditional cathedral-like space, one with candles and confessionals—one that called me to it.

After brunch one day, she invited me to attend her church in the Old Northside area of Indianapolis. She explained it was culturally diverse, and she loved the priest. I agreed to attend the following weekend. I was speechless when we parked that next Sunday. We were right in front of the same church I'd walked to up the street from our old duplex, the one I'd felt calling me to come inside. This was it. I walked in and immediately felt like I'd found home.

For about eighteen months, I arrived early to Mass. I prayed and gave thanks for the man who would enter my life. I visualized all the attributes he would have, always thinking back to my list. With each attribute I thought of, I gave genuine heartfelt thanks to God for delivering this man when I was ready for him.

As I began to imagine officially joining the Catholic church, I felt conflicted. I knew my family wouldn't respond well and my old church friends definitely wouldn't like it. I'd been raised to believe Catholicism in general was simply wrong. I'd once brought a Catholic friend with me to my childhood church, and upon filling out her visitor card, the sermon became about how Catholics were essentially anti-Christ. Even my father had somehow gotten sucked into a conspiracy that the pope himself was the anti-Christ.

My time in the Catholic church made me long for a greater sense of belonging. For nine months, I attended weekly classes for RCIA (Right of Christian Initiation for Adults) to officially become Catholic. In joining RCIA, I became a "candidate," also called a "catechumen." The rituals and the mystery of Catholicism drew me in. The stillness was a far cry from the overly produced theater-like church services I had once attended.

At the end of RCIA, I began participating in the initiation rites: reconciliation (confession), baptism (since I couldn't find my baptismal records), confirmation (being confirmed into the church), and Eucharist (receiving of the body and blood of Christ). With every mystery I learned, I developed an increasing hunger for more mystery.

The Thursday of Holy Week arrived, and it took me back to my first memory of communion. Maundy Thursday is when soon-to-be converts participate in a ceremony where the priest washes the foot of the catechumen in front of the congregation. Humility consumed me as I choked back tears.

My next step was the right of reconciliation. Because I'd already been baptized, I'd make my confession before Easter Vigil. As I prepared for confession, I was flooded with memories of every bad deed I'd done, and I experienced my first look at Catholic guilt. But I wanted to be stronger than my guilt. The priest had spoken to us before Holy Week and explained that for confession, we could keep a veil between us or could opt to speak face-to-face. When it was my turn, I knelt, looked at the prayer in front of me, and threw back the veil. The priest looked at me with a little shock and said, "You know you don't have to have the veil pulled back, right?"

"I do," I replied. "I figure if I can't confess my sins to you face-to-face, then what am I going to do when I meet God and have to give an account?"

"Okay," he said. "Let's continue, then."

My sins poured out of me, the deepest and darkest ones I hadn't shared with anyone. And the compassion I received resulted in such a deeply healing peace. Man's laws, the laws I'd been taught as a child about confessing to another human instead of God, were struck down in my mind at that moment.

Easter Vigil arrived, a night rich in ceremony, tradition, and ritual. My dad, my uncle, my aunt, my two cousins, and Polina came to witness my confirmation.

Entering the church with candles and chanting in the dark with the other catechumen, I felt like I belonged to something bigger than myself. As the time for the Eucharist approached, the choir began to sing the Litany of the Saints. I had adopted the name of Saint Veronica, chosen because of the simple and humble way she served Christ as he was on his way to be crucified. As I listened to the song, tears rolled down my cheeks. They were tears of relief—of having found my own way to a faith of my choosing—and gratitude for belonging.

This new freedom allowed me to feel unrestricted in other ways too—food included. I had been abusing my body with junk food, and I felt my body telling me what I was eating was making me feel like crap. But even after I removed junk from my diet, I slowly crept toward three hundred pounds. Additionally, I'd noticed for some time that my fingernails were detaching from their nailbeds, and doctors couldn't tell me what was wrong. So, I sought out help from manicurists since they see fingernails all day, every day, but the only answer I got was that it didn't look like a fungus, which was a relief, but nobody knew what was causing it.

Around this same time, one of the women I worked with at the timeshare exchange company was getting ready to go through bariatric surgery. The more she shared about the procedure, the more intrigued I became. I talked to other gastric bypass patients to get their feedback on the surgery, their recovery, and their results. I also spoke with a friend and his wife who went through the lap band procedure, a less invasive option. After attending a half-day seminar, I thought I'd found my golden ticket, and I opted for the bariatric sleeve procedure. It was the safest permanent solution that would fix my obesity while considering factors like fertility and my social life.

I had the surgery, and my dad took me home once it was deemed safe for me to be discharged. That night I spiked a fever reaching almost 104 degrees, so I returned to the hospital.

This routine went on for two straight months. For two months I wasn't home for more than two days. I spent Thanksgiving, my birthday, and Christmas that year in the hospital. I had three surgeries for post-op infection, contracted C. diff, and had no less than six esophagrams to determine why food and liquid immediately refluxed into my esophagus. I had two pic lines placed because my veins hide and roll, and they ran out of places to poke me. I also had a feeding tube for close to two weeks because I simply couldn't eat and keep anything down. After the first few days on the feeding tube, I noticed my nails were reconnecting to my nail beds. Nutrition—this was what was causing my problem! Over the two weeks I was on the feeding tube, my nails looked healthier than they had in over a decade.

When I was finally healthy enough to go home, I followed the rules about food. I never drank soda, ate bread, or ate more than eight ounces of food at a time. While my nail health degraded a little bit, they no longer were on the verge of falling off, and in my book, that was a win. My appetite was entirely gone, though. I didn't want to eat because I was afraid of throwing up, and I was tired of throwing up. So, my surgeon prescribed me a medication to help, and it worked. Too well. I went to the store and bought three kinds of cookies, two bags of chips, and my first post-op surgery soda, Root Beer.

Enough was enough. It was time to live a new life. A healthy balance of exercise, better food choices, and moderation caused my body to begin to shrink before my eyes. By this time I'd left the timeshare exchange company, which was rife with high school shenanigans, and I'd started working in the medical field sterilizing surgical instruments. The job required instruments to be cleaned and sterilized meticulously, and I found such satisfaction in it. I'd always wanted to work in the medical field, and this job placed me right where I needed to be to learn if I wanted to actually pursue it.

Because I had dropped about seventy pounds, I fit into medium scrubs, and I was *feelin' good*. I was cute, and I rocked those blue scrubs fiercely. Unfortunately, those pounds started to return almost as quickly as they'd left me. And within a year, I started having crippling pelvic pain, intensely sharp pain that doubled me over. These bouts were usually short-lived, lasting only thirty minutes to an hour, but occasionally, I would be debilitated for days. On the job, I'd find myself lying face down on the floor of our sterile processing break-room. I prayed that the heating pad under my lower abdomen would get the pain to stop. Thank God for the compassionate nurses and other medical workers working there. But once again, I was left with no medical explanation for my pain.

After about a year and a half at the hospital, I could feel the call to entrepreneurship pulling me back to it. I gave my notice but agreed to work as needed on an on-call basis. Since I had a little more free time, I began spending nights out with my high school girlfriends. We frequented an outdoor athenaeum that had live music, a great atmosphere, and tons of liquor. It was there I ran into Simon's family. Simon, my first love. I asked if it would be appropriate for me to contact him. They said yes, and after decades apart, I finally got to mend my heart from the time he broke it when I was a young teenager. I very pointedly asked him what would make him flip a switch and hurt me like that.

"Your dad made it very clear that if anything happened between us sexually that I would be jailbait."

Jailbait—not *gel bait*! Everything made sense. What I didn't know at the time was that my parents didn't love the age difference between us. My mom didn't love the "dark side" of Simon, and if I had to guess, I'd say my dad thought about what happened when he dated my mom—how he'd gotten her, a girl four years younger, pregnant when she was seventeen. Then the minister at church (or his wife) leaked the announcement they were expecting, and they were ridiculed.

Although I was open to it at first, Simon and I didn't reconcile. Too much time and circumstance had changed the people we could have been together.

Soon after working in my own business again, Dee, the fine man at the timeshare company, started DMing me on social media. It was a welcome surprise. He was friendly, with shades of flirty. We slowly got to know more about each other. He enjoyed refurbishing furniture, so he sent pictures of his finished pieces. He teased me about my fear of spiders. I teased him about his hatred of feet. Excited about his new home, he proudly shared all his home updates and renovations with me.

A couple months passed, and I got an invitation to his housewarming party. This man, who I'd have done somersaults to date a few years prior, invited me to his party! It felt like we'd been connecting over the past months, but in my mind, I couldn't believe it to be true. I mean, why would he be interested in me? Nah, certainly not.

I agreed to go, and as our messaging continued over the next couple weeks, it became a little clearer to me there may, in fact, be a spark. It was unmistakable, really. Then the day of his housewarming party arrived, and it just so happened it was the same day as an Indianapolis Colts game I had tickets for. My nerves were SHOT, and all my inner saboteurs kicked in.

Let's find a way to kill this thing before it even has a chance to start. You're not worthy of a man like him. You're going to make a fool of yourself.

I got on Facebook Messenger before the Colts game. "Hey, don't think I'll be able to make it to your housewarming party tonight," I typed. "I didn't realize it was going to be the same day as the Colts game that I've already committed to going to."

His reply caused me to spiral.

"Amber, I've lived in Indianapolis for thirteen years. Do you really think I'd have my housewarming party at the same time as the Colts game? I allowed plenty of time after the game was over for everyone to get here. If you don't want to come, fine. Don't come."

All the bells and sirens went off in my head. "Red alert! Red alert! You're blowing it, woman!" I apologized profusely and arrived about fifteen minutes before the housewarming party began. He was in an old T-shirt and black jogging pants, wrapping scallops and shrimp in bacon.

"Have a seat over there. Make yourself comfortable." I was one of three people who had arrived early. I sat on the barstool in the kitchen, just fidgeting and constantly asking what I could do to help. "You're my guest. You don't have to do anything." But after I asked a couple more times, he caved. "Okay. I bought all the stuff to make appletinis. It's in the basement at the bar. You used to be a bartender, right?" I did. And I had a job to keep my brain occupied. I was hoping this would keep me from ruining my chances with him.

That night, I kept everyone's glass full, but limited myself to only a couple drinks since my bariatric surgery made alcohol's impact hit me quicker. We were all having an incredible time. Then, as Michael Jackson's "Billie Jean" began playing, Dee headed downstairs. An open space on the basement floor and libations led to lowered inhibitions. His feet moved like the Michael I'd seen glide across the stage in 1983. And not just the moonwalk, either. He could really dance. Be still my heart! I'd always wanted to date someone who loved to dance as much as I did. I joined him, and our chemistry was immediate.

After the dancing was over for the night, I decided to leave so as to not overstay my welcome. I leaned in for a kiss, only to land my lips squarely on his nose! Despite the awkwardness of that moment, I'm so grateful Dee snapped me out of my hesitation that day. One of the best decisions of my life was going to his housewarming party.

With a dating history that led me to look for red flags, I was surprised when I didn't find any when Dee and I started officially seeing each other. I was even more surprised when he was more than okay with truly courting me. On our first official date, he took me to see Dave Chappelle, second row. I wasn't used to this sort of treatment. I had been the one who had done all the planning of special moments in my previous relationships.

Before the show, we went to one of my favorite German restaurants in Indianapolis. We shared more about who we were and what brought us to where we were in that moment. When he began telling me about his previous marriage and its eventual demise, I was floored. He took responsibility for how he had contributed to it. No excuses. Just accountability. My heart skipped a beat. It was as if the man I'd waited for all these years was sitting right in front of me. "Why couldn't I have found you about five years ago?" I asked.

"Oh, you wouldn't have liked the person I was at that time. Trust me. Timing is everything." We agreed to be grateful to have found each other at exactly the right time.

Later, as we waited in line to get into the show, freezing our asses off in the Midwest winter cold, we talked for probably close to an hour. We discussed our faith and spiritual journeys. We shared a little about our families, the big and small moments from our childhood. We were off to a good start.

Over the next few months, we spent countless hours communicating. We took time to really get to know one another, and within six months, we moved in together. Not long after, I noticed a rhythm to my pelvic pain. Two weeks before I'd get my period, the pain would begin. For two straight weeks, I would have intense sporadic bursts of crippling pain, rendering me totally unable to move. My period would come, and the pain would disappear. I saw a gynecologist who did multiple laparoscopies to see if it was endometriosis. He found and cleared adhesions in my fallopian tubes, but still, the pain continued. Perhaps it was adhesions from my bariatric surgery?

I saw my bariatric surgeon and he agreed they can be quite painful and may be the cause of my pain. I had a procedure, and an hour after we returned home from the surgery, as I lay on the couch eating saltines and drinking water, I heard a pop in my lower abdomen. Fear paralyzed me.

"Dee! Um . . . I just heard something pop in my tummy."

The look on his face gave him away. "Should we take you to the ER?"

I had an inner knowing that this was urgent. After entering the ER, I was rushed back into surgery. Apparently, during the first surgery, my bowel had been nicked. Over the course of three days, I had four surgeries to repair my bowel and figure out the source of the infection causing my soaring temperature. At one point, they weren't sure whether I was going to make it. But I rallied and pulled through, my boyfriend by my side the whole time.

My recovery was long. After I was deemed healthy once more, Dee quit his job at the timeshare exchange company. We then traveled to Florida to visit family and get away for a few days. There, Dee saw me light up in a way he'd never seen before.

"You really love the ocean, don't you?"

"I do. When I was eighteen, I traveled to Florida with my parents and my brother. He and my parents were arguing, and I just wanted some peace, so I grabbed my CD Walkman and walked out to the beach. I laid on a beach chair that night, just listening to the ocean. It was so peaceful. I slid the headphones over my ears and listened to The Brian Setzer Orchestra as I watched lightning strike the water off in the distance. I've never felt peace like that. Now, every time I come to Florida, I go to the beach at night."

A few days later, as we sat out on the balcony of our condo looking out at the ocean, Dee looked at me and said, "Why don't we move here?" I laughed it off, but he was serious. So, he put his house up for sale. Our plan had been to move to an apartment for a year while we traveled to and from Florida in search of our future home, but that apartment fell through at the last minute, so Dee, our dog, our cat, and I had to find somewhere to move within two days. Thankfully, my former boss and soul sister, Polina, let us use her basement as our temporary home.

A few months later, I reached out to my good friend Jamie. He was dating a man who lived in the area of Florida where we were looking to move. I remembered him telling me that this man, Terrence, had a relative who was a realtor there. Within a few weeks, I was on my way to Florida with my dad to house hunt, while Dee stayed behind with our animals. But after two solid days of house hunting, nothing really stood out to me. Dad and I decided to stay one more night, and the next morning, I woke up to a text from our realtor.

"There's a house that's been on the market for a couple of months. This morning, they reduced it to just over your budget. I'll bet if we make an offer at your max budget, they'll take it. Would you like me to set up an appointment to go see it?"

It didn't have everything I wanted, but it was cute enough and suited our needs. As I was qualifying for the mortgage, my company was doing white-label marketing work for a large agency in Indianapolis. As if qualifying for a mortgage while being self-employed isn't hard enough, two of my contracts ended and the large agency changed its business model, a move that caused me to lose all my income right before we bought our home. Not ideal.

After a few months in Florida, Dee and I had used up our savings. New house, new mortgage, a new state, and no money—it wasn't exactly a winning combination. I got on a call with Jamie again. He worked for an industry-leading telecom company, and I thought maybe he could help me get a job that paid a decent salary. Thankfully, I was hired because of the results I'd achieved for my marketing strategy clients. With a career boasting a laundry list of wins, I was brought on because they knew I could market in a way most of their traditional sales team couldn't: digitally.

After about three months of being on the sales team, I'd started to really find my groove. I was networking virtually before it really became the norm. But even though I was hitting 500 percent of my goal in this role, I was being micromanaged and harassed beyond belief. Instead of handwritten notes left on my workstation by a grateful boss who cared about me as a person, I was bombarded with hourly check-in calls asking me where I was, daily roll call sales meetings, and a never-ending push for more sales.

One day, when my boss came to my cubicle and saw me marketing digitally (because that's the entire reason they hired me), they told me I had to go out and start knocking on doors. Despite exceeding sales goals and getting results, nothing was ever enough. I packed up my laptop, headed to my car, and heard my phone ring. It was my boss again. The same boss who had just shooed me out of the office to go door knock three minutes earlier was calling to find out where I went.

Earlier that morning I had woken up chewing on pieces of my teeth I must have ground off in my sleep that night. It was clear this job was literally going to kill me if I didn't get out. But I was worried about money. I called Dee in tears. "I can't do this anymore." I explained what had happened, and Dee told me to quit. He told me we'd figure it out, just like we always did.

The next day, I pulled into the parking lot, put my phone into its holder on my dashboard, and told God and anyone who would listen that I was finished with this type of employment. No one should be treated the way I had. I knew what it meant to be treated well on a job, and this wasn't it. Thankfully, Tasha, one of the women who'd seen me announce on social media that I was quitting my job, reached out to me. She'd been in Stuart, Florida, for a long time and knew everyone on the Treasure Coast. My gutsy move to announce my departure from the corporate world caught her eye. She messaged me on Facebook and asked if we could meet up for coffee. I don't think she knew how dire her message was for me. We met up to brainstorm ways to overcome the obstacles we all faced, to celebrate when we had a win, and to simply share time together.

"When I left Indiana, it was common practice there to show up for one another in business. If you needed a connection, all you needed to do was reach out to another business owner from our network and they had your back," I said. "When I first arrived in Florida, I attended five networking events in one day and was floored. It was 'bro-centric' networking, full of rules about who could pitch and who couldn't. If you could pitch, you had thirty seconds to do so, then you listened to a hundred other people give their pitch, and finally, you had about thirty minutes at the end to rub elbows with 'the right people.'"

Tasha listened well, hearing me out.

"Those five networking meetings had 90 percent of the same people, most of them already cliqued up, and it just didn't feel like anything I wanted to be a part of. All I want is a small group of friends who will be direct with me and that I don't have to tiptoe around. I'm extroverted around my people, but around everyone else, it causes me a lot of anxiety."

She sat back, took a deep breath, and empathized as giant tears began forming in my eyes. She knew exactly the person for me. Tasha introduced me to a woman who would turn out to be one of my best friends and mentors, Lisa. She also invited me to be a volunteer for an annual event that helps people bring about the abundance they seek in life. Based on the state of affairs in my life at that point, words like *manifest* and *intention* had disappeared from my vocabulary. I was no longer intentional about much of anything. I was in survival mode.

I accepted Tasha's invitation to be a volunteer who kept time for the speakers while they were on stage, and as I simultaneously participated in the event, I lit the manifestation fire within me once again. Tasha talked about holding a thought, turning that thought into a visualization, showing gratitude for what you wished as if you had it right now, and waiting for your manifestation to show up. For three days, I showed up. For three days, I came home and shared with Dee what I'd learned. She sparked hope in me for the first time in a long time. And that spark became a flame.

I was determined I would create the type of networking group I wanted to be a part of, a place where women could show up and not be competitively minded but supportive in the knowledge that there's plenty of room for everyone at the table. I started a Facebook group: Women Business Owners Supporting Women Business Owners. In it, I taught women how to network in a new way.

Almost immediately after expressing my dream, I manifested a client in Florida who'd actually expressed interest before we'd left Indiana. A significant contract started the ball rolling. A contract paying double the original came in soon after. Dee and I were down to our last $1,800 in savings, and I needed a miracle. After talking with Dee, we decided we'd spend the $1,800 on my sales coach, Laura.

During our first call, she asked me, "If you could do anything in life and make money doing it, what would you do?"

"I'd just make connections with people who need each other."

Soon, I had one contract, and then another, and our choice was paying off. I was intentional about meditating daily, journaling after I meditated, and then closing my eyes and visualizing that journal prompt being my current reality. Soon enough, we were back to living comfortably.

My first marriage had been annulled a couple years earlier by the church due to the persuasion of my mother to get married so early. Now, Dee's first marriage had also been annulled. Dee took a job at a telecommunications company in management, and together, we were financially stable enough to throw the St. Paddy's Day wedding and party that we both wanted.

I was remarried, and my professional life was taking off. Life was finally looking up, but it was clear I couldn't keep onboarding clients while I was suffering my ongoing and crippling pelvic pain. No matter how long the pain lasted, it zapped every bit of energy from my body, and the only thing I could do was rest and pray for the pain to stop. I chose not to take painkillers because the opiate crisis was at its peak, so I suffered through. Plus, I couldn't walk into a doctor's office and say shit about pain without getting the side-eye, so I didn't. I kept quiet, literally gritted my teeth, and bore it all until I couldn't do it for one more minute.

I went to three gynecologists in Florida before I found one who would both listen to me and meet my needs. I was hopeful when my first gynecologist ordered a number of tests, including a saline sonogram. "The doctor who performs and reads your test is the best doctor of sonography in the state of Florida, so if she says you don't have adenomyosis, you don't have it," she told me confidently.

I didn't get a diagnosis from her but did get that same side-eye I got from every other doctor I'd told about my pain. "It could just be cysts. They can cause pain. Take Naproxen if you have pain." I clearly wasn't getting anywhere with her.

My next gynecologist was hell-bent on selling me some MLM supplements, then spoke sharply to me when I decided to stop taking them. But at least he gave me hope that a diagnosis was within reach. He was relatively certain I did have adenomyosis and wanted to do an open hysterectomy that would have me in recovery for weeks.

From my time working at the hospital in the surgical department, it occurred to me that robotic surgeries were becoming more popular due to their low recovery time, so I found a gynecologist who specialized in them. I'd seen enough hospitals in the past decade, and I had no desire to spend another night in one after an open hysterectomy. I was in and out following the robotic surgery, and after three days, I was feeling almost no pain. In two weeks, I was back to life as usual—but without the debilitating pain. The prognosis? Adenomyosis—a condition that occurs when the endometrial tissues grow into the wall of the uterus—just as I'd suspected.

After my short recovery, it was important for me to keep doing what I needed to do to feel good in my body. I'd signed up for weekly chiropractic treatments to keep my spine aligned and my central nervous system healthy. While I wasn't the heaviest I'd ever been post-surgery, I also knew I could be feeling better from a health perspective.

A few months prior to my hysterectomy, I'd reached out to a friend of mine who did massage therapy and lymphatic drainage post-surgery. I'd noticed that her profile photo on Facebook had changed; it looked like she had dropped a considerable amount of weight. I was curious, but knowing she'd beaten cancer, I wanted to broach the topic with care just in case the weight loss was medically related.

I connected with her, told her she looked great, then complimented her on a job well done. She thanked me, so I felt like it was safe to ask her how she had lost the weight. I was surprised by her answer. She told me she had accomplished it through meditation. I was confused, but thought heck, if I could meditate and look as great as she did, I'd give it a shot. Meditation with an overactive brain is a feat, but I found a great app called Unplug that had quick and easy guided secular meditations. I didn't notice anything earth-shattering at first, but my days seemed to be a bit easier and less stressful.

Then one day after I started meditating, on my way to my chiropractor's office, I heard an inner voice as I was passing the retirement community where my dad lives: *If you don't want to suffer the same fate as your mom, you need to see an endocrinologist. She was having some of the same symptoms you're having now, and she ignored them.*

At that time, I had no idea what an endocrinologist even did. Following my chiropractor appointment, I began researching, but I kept finding information that had to do with diabetes. My mom hadn't died from diabetes, so what could this inner voice have been suggesting? I called my dad to ask, but I gave him a very tame version of what I'd heard, as he's leery of hearing or seeing spirits. I asked him whether my mom had a lot of the same symptoms I'd been having, and he confirmed she'd had.

The more I researched, the more I learned the role of the pancreas and its function in regulating hormones that control blood sugar. I was flabbergasted. I felt as if I might actually be on to something. I researched endocrinologists within a thirty-mile radius of where I lived and found one who seemed promising, so I made an appointment.

After looking at my bloodwork, looking at my skin, and doing a general checkup, she immediately diagnosed me with Hashimoto's Thyroiditis and Polycystic Ovary Syndrome (PCOS). I quickly let her know I'd had my ovaries removed during my hysterectomy and assumed that she was trying to over-diagnose me. She countered my objection with a kind but confident retort: "That's a common misconception. PCOS is an autoimmune disorder that often affects the ovaries. It's not a disorder of the ovaries."

I was prescribed a thyroid medication, plus one for PCOS. I also found out I was prediabetic and that I should try to control it with food and movement to avoid being put on medication for diabetes. I added poultry and fish back into my diet, and I only consumed whole foods. I removed gluten and focused on low-glycemic fruits and vegetables. I started walking a few times a day. After three months, my A1C (the test that measures your average blood sugar over a period of three months) dropped below the prediabetic level.

CHAPTER 8:
AMBER'S EVIDENCE

As a teenager, while going through years of fad diets, I remember having a certain "knowing" that I had a thyroid problem, but my doctor did a test that came back normal. How was I supposed to know to push him harder to do more thorough testing? When I later spoke to a naturopathic doctor, she explained that the typical panel they do to check thyroid health is like checking the radiator fluid to see if your oil levels are right.

Even today, when it seems like we've made so many advancements in technology and equality, women's voices go unheard and are dismissed in the medical field, even by female doctors whom we would expect to better listen. It is our responsibility to show up for ourselves—from listening to our intuition, to following the breadcrumbs, to connecting the medical dots, to being our own health advocates and finding out answers. It is also our responsibility to do something with that information once we find those answers.

As for me, I finally understood what my friend meant when she told me about using meditation to achieve her goals. There's a power that gets unleashed when we quiet the noise around us. Some people think it's the space where we can hear God. Others believe it's when our higher selves or our consciousness can be heard. I heard that consciousness. I followed the trail. I got silent again. And again. And it was there I found my purpose. It was there I became truly unleashed. When you know your purpose and it aligns with your passion, your path is set aflame, and you will do *anything* to make sure that purpose gets fulfilled.

That's not to say there will be no bumps in the road—we just become keenly attuned to what those bumps mean. It's in the moments of stillness that our "stuff" is made known. Growing up poor, and only seeing people who were materialistic (or just total assholes), gave me many subconscious limiting beliefs about money. Being valued based on appearances made me not love myself—so my subconscious started to sabotage my body by treating it poorly.

Many people would probably agree that 2020 was a year of transformation for them. For me, it was one of my biggest transformative years. It brought my holy trinity of events— ridding my body of chronic pelvic pain, receiving my diagnosis and developing a treatment plan, and toying with the idea of writing this book. These were the catalysts to profound growth.

My Facebook group grew to 1,000 members, and within six months, it hit 15,000. Every other post I approved in the group was one in which women were panicking and worrying about losing their businesses. Thus, I was literally thrust into women's leadership. I took note of the needs of the women flocking to my group. I invited all backgrounds of spiritual leaders to guide in prayer or meditation to help ease our collective and individual anxiety. I invited professionals in their fields to share expertise to help the women make it through, though not unchanged. I took time to meet hundreds of women, to build connections, and to connect my new network to my existing one. The number one goal I told my sales coach, Laura, was to get paid to simply connect people. And it was happening!

After learning more about the women in my group, I began digging in and doing research about small businesses. That lit a flame in me to move from a more passive role into an active one in supporting women-owned businesses. I decided to start Shop From Her. Shop From Her strives to be a movement of people who make the decision to shop and hire consciously instead of doing what is easiest or even cheapest.

It was during this time of stepping into my purpose that Lynn, one of the women I met when I got back into marketing full time, reached out to me. I'd seen an invitation on Facebook, welcoming me to a group where we could follow along the process of writing her "book baby." I shared my enthusiasm and support for this journey, as I knew it wouldn't be an easy one given the topic: the process of caring for her terminally ill mother.

Soon enough we were on the phone, and she filled me in on how she found her publisher. After sharing my own vision for a book, she encouraged me to reach out and gather more information. After saying yes to my publisher, I felt an energetic shift. So much of my life I'd lived in a state of victimization and martyrdom, neither of which I planned on being a part of going forward. If I was going to write a book, it was going to be my opportunity to use my voice to share my story. Not a story of tragedy, but one of triumph.

Making a shift from tragedy to triumph doesn't simply happen with a decision, though. It happens with a decision and, as my friend Tasha calls it, inspired action. In order to gain clarity on that inspiration, there was a lot of inner work I needed to do. Following that inner voice when my subconscious was consumed with trauma made for a version of me centered in ego. My actions and reactions were often centered in fear, and it was beginning to take its toll.

There was so much to undo, to untether myself from. But I wasn't really encouraged to deal with my traumas. In our faith, forgiveness is often thought to be the vehicle to healing. Forgiveness, however, doesn't undo damage. It simply allowed me to move forward without wishing revenge or ill-will on another person. The traumas were still there, lying under the surface, pushed down—exactly where I'd left them when I made the decision not to deal with them. It was a perfect storm to create big illnesses like strokes and cardiovascular disease. So, I made up my mind it was time to confront the pain, head on.

I'd heard about a number of different shamanic-led journeys that helped guide others to find radical healing. I opted to try one. It was yet another chance for me to step outside of my comfort zone by embarking on a journey and a path that had been labeled "witchcraft" in the church where I was raised, and in many subsequent churches thereafter.

I received instructions to follow a specific diet that would raise my energetic vibration, and upon studying the science behind it, it was legitimate. "Keep a journal the week before your journey. Write down what comes up for you, what fears you want to release, and what you intend to receive as a result of your participation in this journey." I followed the directions perfectly. I showed up on the day of the journey with my journal in hand, intentions set. The shaman gave a blessing, protected our space, told me what to expect, and off I went.

It was during this journey I unmistakably "heard" the inaudible voice of the Creator. Communicating through thoughts, I was shown the beauty of everything surrounding me. How the trees, grass, and even the tiny inchworm that had made its way next to my blanket were all purposefully interwoven. Each of us feeding the next in all ways. I had met what I'd heard referred to as God, but the "God" I grew up knowing was in a box much too small for the presence I spent time with on this journey.

Knowing the value of all things gave me the momentum I needed to really dig in and see the beauty in myself. To see that beauty, I knew I had to undo a lifetime of ugly first. I sought out a shaman who focused on healing the mother wound. Another shamanic journey ensued as I journeyed to the depths of my own inner landscape: my subconscious. It was there I found a wounded five-year-old, completely untrusting of the adult, albeit an older version of herself, who approached her. I spent more time with that young soul day after day, week after week, until I earned her trust. I started to reparent her, and to earn her trust, so that that same trust would flood into my own life. After a year in that space, it was time for a break.

I got another nudge nearly a year later to do one more shamanic journey, similar to the first I'd done, but with a different intention: "What is my purpose and how should I show up during my time on Earth?" That same "God" voice answered. It called me out on my bullshit, how I show up and how I hide, how I react when I'm triggered, and how cute it is that I think I'm in control. We even laughed together, completely stripped of ego. And then it happened. The intention I set was revealed to me.

I was whisked through a dark tunnel expeditiously. The closer I got to the end of that tunnel, the brighter the light got. When I reached the end, there in front of me was the brightest yellowish-orange light I had ever seen. It suddenly burst open and the form of a female figure, made of the same golden light, floated in front of me.

"Who is that?" I asked.

"You wanted to know what your purpose is and how you were to show up. This is you. You are a powerful creator, and everything you need is already within you."

The love and light emanating from the being was intoxicating. It was the most beautiful and peaceful thing I'd ever seen. I began to sob from the pit of my soul, and in that moment, I fell wholly in love with my spirit. A roar of grief poured from my diaphragm for the years that light had been hidden and for the release of gratitude for the second half of my life. I made a vow to let that light shine unabashedly and without repression from the millions of people who don't want others to know this light lives in each one of us.

We are all cocreators of the lives we live, individually and collectively. While every trauma we experience may not be our fault, I realized it was my responsibility to actively heal and to give others permission to do the same. It was this journey that primed my path to living a life more intentionally. I would no longer consume fear-based content being hurled through traditional media sources and social media, and I would limit my time listening to conspiracy theories that could lead me down rabbit holes that lead to madness. While I'm not so blind as to think everything we're fed is truth, the question becomes "If this conspiracy is true, then what?" The answer in most instances is "Not a damn thing."

I intentionally chose to change what I could change in front of me in that moment. I chose to build a safe space for those who are in alignment with creating their hopes and dreams. I chose to control my inner world and to bring peace by bringing my light to humans and the world. And that inner peace became a mirror—through the looking glass—to my outer world. Peace is now my most sought-after currency, and love is the air I breathe. Anything outside of that isn't feeding the light I spent time with on my journey.

My group grew to nearly 35,000 women business owners globally (or those striving to own a business). How did I do it? By intentionally choosing who I spent my time with. By serving others. And by finally giving myself permission to see the power of the Creatrix I am at my very core.

I was given one test after another to stand in my power, and while that statement sounds empowering, they were true trials for the formerly soft-spoken, timid girl who let people walk all over her. I went to therapy again, mostly because I felt guilty about cutting people off who flooded my life with unhealthy and toxic behaviors. I silenced the voices of patriarchal oppression telling me I couldn't be this or it was a sin to be that.

I dug in and learned the historical and political "advances" made during times of theological and philosophical change. And it was then it became clear to me—that light is the voice that will always guide me where I need to be. That light doesn't provoke guilt or shame. It provides guidance, instills peace, and lights the path home to self-love. I got still and listened to that still-small voice inside of me, and that voice steadily grows to this day.

Throughout the pandemic, to continue healing, Dee and I spent every single night (when weather allowed) outside on our patio. Instead of sitting in front of the television, we were outside with nature, communing, and allowing it to teach us by observing the subtle nuances.

I drew swallow-tailed kites to me. Watching them float effortlessly through the sky, I took note of their flexibility, their agility, and the playfulness they had. To me, it seemed, while they may be hunting or scouting, play was always inter-twined. I also watched how the palm tree to the right of our patio danced, bowed, and swayed with the strongest of winds without breaking, teaching me to honor Mother Nature and all her resources.

Dee and I began to speak about our future, using the tools we'd been taught—some from the Bible, some from inner knowledge, and some from other readings. We literally planned our life, without knowing how everything would play out, by speaking it into existence.

"What will Shop From Her be, really?" Dee asked me one night.

"It's going to have multiple components. Women will be able to network in an authentic and genuine way. We'll be able to teach one another basic skills to build our businesses. We'll be able to buy from one another and promote each other on social media channels. We'll be able to consciously decide who to buy from instead of just buying from whomever is top of mind. I'm going to make shopping consciously become top of mind. Oh! And we'll do a tour. We'll buy an RV and travel around the US and Canada first. We'll schedule times to be in different cities, and I will interview these women about their businesses. I'll select people who need help with their marketing and make that part of the interview."

"Let's talk about what the RV will look like," Dee then said.

We'd taken a formal process of visualization and made it a part of our everyday life, with ease and anticipation. We spent countless hours drawing with our minds exactly the future we wanted to live. Being intentional with our time—even if that intentionality led to playtime—was the most transformative habit we developed.

The small voice inside me gave me permission to freely express who I am. Instead of relying on friends and family, the people I'd been taught I needed to depend on to survive, I surrounded myself with those who were genuinely ecstatic to see me transforming from the caterpillar hiding in my cocoon from the world to the butterfly breaking free and untying the ropes that had kept me oppressed for most of my life.

I recalled a conversation between a confused little girl and a caterpillar. Seared into my memory were Alice's words about thinking she knew who she was, but after everything changed she wasn't so sure. . . .

In a structure like a cult where women's voices are silenced, it can be difficult to break free from the stronghold it has. My meditation time allowed me to shatter that stronghold, bit by bit. I now work with women who have a message to share with the world but don't know how to reach the masses.

When we are asked to wear a mask, to show up as anything or anyone outside our authentic selves, we create disharmony in our body. Disowning a part of who we are tells our inner self we don't appreciate or love that side of ourselves. And if we are out of love with the true essence of our being, we start to abuse the machine (our bodies) our spirit inhabits.

And it is for this reason that the scripture from 1 Corinthians 6:19-20 means that we must pay homage to our bodies: "Do you not know that your bodies are temples of the Holy Spirit, who is in you, whom you have received from God?" It is this flesh suit we wear that animates and houses our spirit—a symbiotic connection to the Source of our very being.

How do we treat our bodies like a temple? We educate ourselves about each system function: Our central nervous system (shout out to chiropractors!) and our endocrine system (in my opinion, the two most abused systems because they're the least visible), and every other system in our bodies. Learn how to feed them, how to rest them, how to nurture them. Then our bodies will respond.

Remember that at our very core, we are energy, both physically and spiritually. Learning how to move energy around our bodies has been taught for millennia, but many Christian theologies teach against energy movement like Qi Gong and Tai Chi. Much like witchcraft and shamanism, the church has systematically demonized theologies that threaten its existence. But recognizing myself as an energetic being has changed my life.

In March 2022, Dee and I manifested exactly what we'd been visualizing on our patio during the pandemic. We sold our home for the amount of money we'd visualized. We bought a brand-new travel trailer, known for its quality build and spacious layout, and a 1997 Ford F350 that would make both of my grandfathers' (who were mechanics) hearts happy. This particular truck is known for its "million-mile engine," and it's a rarity.

CHAPTER 9:
FIND YOUR WONDERLAND

No matter how educated or Zen you are, paths to success get harder to climb the closer you get to the top. This has proven to be true in my life, most certainly. In December 2022, after taking a two-year hiatus from mammograms, I felt it was time to get checked. Soon after, I became a member of the titanium clip club. It's not a prestigious membership but one thousands of women undergo yearly. I was notified that during the mammogram, a small spot was detected in my right breast. In a ridiculous turn of events, due to insurance difficulties, it took me five months to get a biopsy. The months of waiting were a test for me, a test to stay in the present and not to spiral down the proverbial rabbit hole into every possible negative scenario. Thankfully, after that five-month wait, the biopsy came and went, and within three days I had the results—I have healthy breasts, and I've never been more thankful for them.

Because I now spend most of my time in Central Florida, I had to find new health-care providers, one of whom was my endocrinologist. As I sat in the empty doctor's office waiting to meet her, I was greeted with a hug by a lovely middle-aged Indian woman with a nose ring shaped like a tiny daisy. "Tell me why you've come to see me, Amber," she asked.

I shared my story about hearing the voice prompting me to see an endocrinologist.

"Ah! That's your inner knowing . . . your intuition! I wish more people would listen to it."

I immediately felt validated.

"So, how has your journey been since starting your treatment plan?"

I explained to her how I had removed gluten and was eating a primarily plant-based, whole-food diet and supplementing it with fish and free-range chicken. As I talked about how I'd been eating lots of fresh organic veggies, fiber, and low carb fruits, tears welled up in my eyes out of the frustration I'd been feeling.

She looked at me empathetically, placed her hand on my shoulder, then patted it. "It's okay. We're going to make it better for you. There is so much hope. Go ahead, tell me more about how things are going."

"No matter what I do, I can't lose weight. I've been on this roller coaster since I was eight years old, and I just want to stop riding it. I want off!"

She took thirty minutes to explain to me what it meant from a total physiological perspective to suffer with insulin resistance. Everything from my high(ish) cholesterol to my fatty liver disease started to make sense. She then placed a glucose monitor on my upper left tricep and told me to leave it there for ten days.

"I have a feeling your bariatric surgery is masking the fact that you are, and have been, type 2 diabetic for a while. But we'll wait to see, and we'll make a treatment plan based on that. You're on the right path. It's a good thing you followed your intuition!"

Three weeks passed, and it was time for my follow-up appointment. She printed out my glucose readings and looked them over. "How do you feel it went?" she asked.

"It was fine," I said. "There were quite a few spikes, and one night the alarm on the meter woke me up due to a very low dip. It took me almost two hours to get it to stabilize."

She confirmed that I did, in fact, have type 2 diabetes and put me on a promising medication that would both keep my blood sugar stabilized and allow me to drop weight. It worked. I began losing weight, and I'm grateful to say I'm absolutely feeling better in my skin.

I know all too well what it's like to have my worth tied up in external thoughts and ideas. I know what it's like to have other people's institutions and ideals forced upon me. I know what it's like to feel like it's my responsibility for how others feel. And I want you to know it's understandable you feel the way you do. But you are not a role. You are not the ideal someone else instills in you. You cannot be put into a box. You are divine, and you are here to cocreate with God (or Source, Spirit, Universe, Creator). And so am I. We're all cocreating our experience together, divinely purposed.

No matter who you are, no matter what background you come from, no matter how much you were loved or not loved, abused or neglected, I need you to know three things: 1) You are not only enough, you are worthy of a good life, whatever that means to you. 2) You deserve to have your voice heard, and you will inevitably face trials in your life. 3) Big shifts happen when your perspective changes from life happening *to you* to life happening *for you*. Yep, even the trials.

As I began to step into my power and my gifts, I was blessed to bring others along with me. As I began to see obstacles as opportunities for growth, I stepped into what's possible instead of living in a state of victimhood. I love the work I do, and I have a talent for spotting the world-changers out there. I intuitively guide thought leaders to grow their own social media audiences. I guide women who have done the deep mental and spiritual work to become ethical influencers so they can grow their affluence and more readily make the changes they hope to see in the world.

Our work together is more than just marketing strategies. Any marketing strategist can help with that. My unique ability is to help my clients break through any mindset barriers that stand in their way to using their voices. When we're afraid of showing up authentically, that fearful energy is sensed by the audience, so I encourage my clients to practice their own "throwing back of the veil," like I did in my first reconciliation, so the world can see exactly who they were sent here to be. Without limitations.

Part of the mindset work is in letting go of the need to people please, the need to be liked, and the need to conform. This was the single hardest obstacle to leap when I decided to write this book. I have been judged. I have been "red-lettered." I've had countless assumptions made about the life I've lived or currently live—most out of ignorance. But those thoughts and assumptions reflect the people making them. It's their own fears and limitations. It is not your responsibility to make others comfortable. It is your responsibility to live—whatever that means to you—and to follow that without apologizing for living fully.

As you start to fully embody your newfound worth, some people, even people you love, will start to resent you. Hear me well. This is not permission to stop shining. This is the next step in your growth. It's your chance to step outside of familial and societal dysfunction and to surround yourself with people who find joy in seeing you thrive. It won't be an easy move, but then growth rarely is. As Thema Davis said, "Refuse to inherit dysfunction. Learn new ways of living instead of repeating what you lived through."

We are the rule breakers, the therapy seekers, the black sheep, the generational trauma healers, and the world-changers. If you feel more hurt than healed, it's time to make moves. It's time to ask yourself what's holding you back and listen to what your higher self tells you. Don't question what you hear. Listen. Untether yourself from what's holding you back and find your wonderland. It's time to change the world.

ACKNOWLEDGMENTS

To my husband, my rock. Thank you for growing with me and for holding space for me to evolve and become a better version of myself. The best gifts you give me daily are your time, patience, encouragement, and love. I am blessed to be your partner in life.

To my dad, who's always encouraged me to think for myself and to push myself. You've given me so many lessons that I'll never forget.

To my mom: I love and appreciate who you were, who you are, and all you had to go through to give me life. Thank you for loving me the best way you knew how.

To my CBFF: thank you for being my first best friend. Thank you for endlessly being footloose with me through our childhood. Thank you for your forgiveness and for your desire to see from another perspective, always.

To my brother: thank you for keeping me laughing, for being a reminder of just how brilliant I am in my own way, and for your patience and acceptance as I discover exactly who I am.

To my closest circle of friends—you know who you are: thank you for loving me and encouraging my goofy ass to just be who I am. The gift of acceptance is healing and it's priceless.

And finally, to Ben and Polina for showing the meaning of agape love. I don't know what I would have done without you.

www.ingramcontent.com/pod-product-compliance
Lightning Source LLC
Chambersburg PA
CBHW071152120626
46546CB00006B/2235